PENGUIN BOOKS

CITIES OF VESUVIUS

MICHAEL GRANT has been successively Chancellor's medallist and fellow of Trinity College, Cambridge, Professor of Humanity at Edinburgh University, first Vice-Chancellor of Khartoum University, and President and Vice-Chancellor of the Queen's University of Belfast. Until 1966 he was President of the Virgil Society, and was President of the Classical Association in 1977–8. He has also translated Cicero's *Selected Works, Selected Political Speeches, On the Good Life,* and *Murder Trials,* and Tacitus's *Annals of Imperial Rome* for the Penguin Classics: his other books include *The Civilizations of Europe* (1965), *Gladiators* (1967), *Roman Literature, Latin Literature* and *Greek Literature, Cleopatra* (1972), *The Jews in the Roman World* (1973), *The Army of the Caesars* (1974), *The Twelve Caesars* (1975), *The Fall of the Roman Empire* (1976), *Cities of Vesuvius* (1976, Penguin), *Saint Paul* (1976), *Jesus* (1977) and *History of Rome* (1978).

Michael Grant

Cities of Vesuvius:
Pompeii and Herculaneum

PHOTOGRAPHS BY WERNER FORMAN

PENGUIN BOOKS

in association with Weidenfeld and Nicolson

Penguin Books Ltd,
Harmondsworth, Middlesex, England
Penguin Books,
625 Madison Avenue, New York, New York 10022, U.S.A.
Penguin Books Australia Ltd,
Ringwood, Victoria, Australia
Penguin Books Canada Ltd,
2801 John Street, Markham, Ontario, Canada L3R 1B4
Penguin Books (N.Z.) Ltd,
182–190 Wairau Road, Auckland 10, New Zealand

First published in Great Britain by Weidenfeld and Nicolson 1971
First published in the United States of America by
The Macmillan Company 1971
Published in Penguin Books 1976
Reprinted 1978, 1979

Designed by Gerald Cinamon
Maps and plans drawn by Claus Henning

Made and printed in Great Britain by
Butler & Tanner Ltd, Frome and London
Set in Monotype Garamond

Contents

Looking through a monumental gateway, past a fountain
decorated with a head of Medusa, into the Triangular
Forum of Pompeii

Preface

1,892 years ago, within the space of a very few catastrophic hours, Pompeii and Herculaneum were overwhelmed by Mount Vesuvius and buried deep down in the earth. But they were not destroyed. Beneath the massive covering which overlaid them, they were preserved, as they would never have been had the disaster not occurred. The peculiar conditions established by ash and mud were such that even the smallest and most fragile objects of daily use have survived. And so that August day, when that whole busy world came to a stop, can be reconstructed in tens of thousands of details, far more completely than any other day that ever happened throughout the whole course of the ancient world. And the many years of existence and development that had gone before the eruption can be reconstructed too.

No mirror of the past could possibly be more vivid than the reflection offered us by Pompeii and Herculaneum; a visit to the two places is an experience that can be paralleled nowhere in the world. In that strange vacuum, its emptiness underlined by innumerable signs of long-arrested activity, life and death seem to be on particularly intimate terms. The smiling countryside all round makes the universal marks of ferocious destruction peculiarly horrifying.

Even the least philosophical of tourists visiting these sites cannot quite escape unfashionable reflections about good and evil, and how they often come together. But he will also not be able to help enjoying himself. For it is another paradox that this apocalyptic scene gives a remarkable amount of pleasure, as it has done for two centuries and more; I shall mention some of the visitors' reactions in the course of this book.

Part of the pleasure derives from a certain feeling of intimacy and recognition: from the realization that these two places, even if grand in certain ways, were very ordinary in others. It is also reassuring, somehow, to see how small they were. We follow the old convention and call them 'cities', and so I have called this book 'Cities of Vesuvius', but the population of both together did not exceed 25,000. Much of their charm, then, lies in this golden mediocrity. However, a good deal also lies in a less cosy reflection, for we are very rapidly forced to conclude that these modest dimensions left room for an infinitely larger number of beautiful things than would be found in almost any town of similar size today. The presence of so many fine paintings, mosaics and sculptures makes one wonder where these tastes came from; and to speculate how far, in this respect, Pompeii and Herculaneum resembled, or differed from, the wider Graeco-Roman world around them. This is an aspect on which some of the books about these towns tend to leave their readers relatively unsatisfied, and I have therefore dwelt on it a little more than usual; though not too much, I hope, because the two sites themselves and the objects that have come from them provide material, even without any such attempts at comparison, which is worth many lifetimes of study.

And indeed those who have written on Pompeii and Herculaneum ever since the exciting days of their first rediscovery, and particularly the men who have devoted years to their investigation on the spot, must come first and foremost in the list of the acknowledgements I have to make. A selection of the more recent works is gratefully included in a list at the end of this book. I also want to express my thanks to Mr Werner Forman for his indispensable collaboration as photographer, to Mr D.E.L. Haynes and Mr Hugh Honour for the benefit of their valuable advice, to Miss Kathy Henderson, Mrs Sandra Bance and Mr Oliver Walston of Messrs Weidenfeld and Nicolson for their editorial organization and aid, and to my wife for her help at every stage of the book.

MICHAEL GRANT
Gattaiola, 1971

I stood within the City disinterred;
    And heard the autumn leaves like light footfalls
Of spirits passing through the streets; and heard
    The mountain's slumberous voice at intervals
Thrill through those roofless halls.
    The oracular thunder penetrating shook
The listening soul in my suspended blood.
    I felt that Earth out of her deep heart spoke ...

SHELLEY, *Ode to Naples*

Overleaf: A man who was suffocated outside the Nucerian Gate, Pompeii. The ash hardened round the corpse so that when there was nothing left of the body its shape was   preserved and could be reconstructed by pouring plaster into the hollow

1. The History of Pompeii and Herculaneum

In western Italy, upon the Tyrrhenian Sea, lies the uniquely inviting land of Campania. This coast, starting a hundred and forty-five kilometres south-east of Rome and extending downwards beyond the Bay of Naples, gave ancient Rome its first good sea-front, its first window upon the Mediterranean, its first idea of becoming a world state. And behind the coast, stretching back to the Apennine range, is a plain which is incredibly favoured by nature. Traversed by two fairly important rivers and fanned by moist south-westerly winds, this territory of spongy volcanic earth, rich in phosphorus and potash, enjoys relatively mild and short winters, and the soil retains enough of the abundant seasonal rainfall to escape ill-effects from three months of summer drought.[1] Campania is alien to the desiccated Italian south – and alien to the modest conceptions of visitors from northern lands. In ancient times, when this was the chief granary of the peninsula, some districts already produced as many as three grain crops every year, in addition, often enough, to a catch-crop of vegetables as well. There were none of the oranges and lemons that can be seen now,[2] but olives and vines grew plentifully, and indeed many of Italy's principal olive groves were in Campania. Walking out of Pompeii today one can see fields bearing vines, fruit-trees and beans at one and the same time. And so it was in antiquity. An extraordinary variety of crops gave constant cover to the fields throughout the year, and yields were perhaps as much as six times higher than the average for the Italian peninsula. And above the plain, for example in the Montes Lactarii (Lattari) at the southern end of the bay, the mountains pastured many thousands of sheep.

'Nothing,' said Madame de Staël, 'gives a more voluptuous idea of life than this climate which intimately unites man to nature.' More than seventeen centuries earlier, the elder Pliny had said much the same; and the Latin writer Florus, though he was a north African who lived in Spain, found Campania the most beautiful place, not only in Italy, but in all the world.[3] And indeed this landscape in the grand style, with its superb sweep of coast, its lush rising shores, its all-enveloping light, its emphatically blue sea and sky, is the perfect illustration of Dr Samuel Johnson's heartfelt assurance that there is nothing that can equal the Mediterranean.

Long before the Romans came, this inviting land had attracted immigrants and invaders. Already in the eighth century BC the Greeks chose Cumae, on the coast just north-west of the bay, for their earliest settlement upon the mainland of Italy. During the two centuries that followed, Cumae exercised widespread control throughout the area, finally becoming one of the main suppliers of grain to other parts of the peninsula. Naples itself, Neapolis, had been settled by Greeks before 650, to judge from reported finds. And then before the end of the sixth century another Greek city was founded next door; this was Dicaearchia, later Puteoli and now Pozzuoli, which in all fields except culture, and particularly in all matters relating to imports and exports, remained more important than Neapolis for hundreds of years.

Puteoli lay 11 kilometres to the west of Neapolis, and the much smaller town of Pompeii was 22 kilometres south-east of Neapolis, almost adjoining the same coast. No doubt even before the Greeks there had been a native Italian (Oscan) fishing and agricultural village or small town on this site, though if so we do not know for how long. But in any case it was supplemented, in due course, by a settlement or trading post of the Greeks. On a tall, southward-facing spur, now known as the Triangular Forum, they built a Doric temple. Its fragmentary remains go back to

Outside the Marine Gate of Pompeii. Tombs are seen in the foreground, and Vesuvius in the background

the sixth century, when the little place was no doubt still under the influence or control of Cumae or Neapolis, forming a staging point on their trade route to the south.

The Greek settlement or post at Pompeii was built on an isolated volcanic ridge about 39 metres above sea-level, produced by a prehistoric flow of lava down the slopes of Vesuvius, which towers up just over eight kilometres away. To the south, beyond where the Greeks built their temple, the flow had stopped abruptly, providing a fortifiable boundary which gave protection against surprise attacks. This cliff-like termination overlooked the river Sarnus (Sarno), which is quite insignificant today but which in ancient times was navigable by ships of respectable tonnage. The shallow-draught vessels of antiquity could anchor in the river itself[4] as well as among the harbour installations of its substantial estuary. The Sarnus, which watered the whole fertile plain south-east of Vesuvius, had already before 700 BC prompted the creation of agricultural villages in the upper reaches of its valley, and not far from the river mouth as well.[5] Then, when Pompeii had been founded, the river meant that the place did not have to depend too much or for too long on the larger harbour-towns, Cumae and Neapolis, that lay to the north. For the Sarnus gave Pompeii the role of sea-port for the adjacent hinterland. And, in particular, it became the port of a native town that lay to the east, eleven kilometres inland, Nuceria Alfaterna (Nocera), an important road centre which drew its wealth from the river plain and dominated the southern regions of Campania.

The Greeks settled not only at Pompeii but at two points on either side of it, both close beside the coast. To the south, at some date unknown, they founded a town at Stabiae, just below the hills at the southern end of the bay. Stabiae, now the shipbuilding town of Castellamare di Stabia, is only five kilometres from Pompeii, and well in sight of its walls. Such proximity meant that Pompeii, in this direction, could never own much land of its own; and indeed its territory did not extend on any side for more than a few kilometres. But the other Greek coastal settlement, to the north of Pompeii, was a good deal smaller still, indeed not one-fifth of its size. This was Heracleion, later to become Herculaneum. Built on a spur projecting from

Pompeii: from a tower in the north wall, looking down past the so-called Arch of Caligula. In the background are the Monti Lattari (Lactarii) at the southern end of the Bay of Naples

View of Herculaneum from the south towards the north-west. On the left is the little colonnade of the House of the Gem, and to its right the House of the Relief of Telephus

the lower slopes of Vesuvius, the little town, extending over something less than twelve hectares, was protected on either flank by ravines containing streams which ran down from the mountain to the sea. The streams were not navigable, and the sea-shore did not boast much of a harbour; nor did any suitable roads lead to the interior. However, Herculaneum served as a minor centre of the coasting trade, and as a transit town on the shore road round the bay. It was only eight kilometres from Neapolis and certain Greek settlers – who probably came from that city – found it worthwhile to establish themselves at Herculaneum at quite an early date. According to a legend it was the hero Heracles (Hercules) himself, returning from Spain, who sacrificed a tithe of his spoils to the gods and created this little town on the spot where his fleet was anchored, naming the foundation after himself.

But in due course a great peninsular power sprang up, and overwhelmed all local interests.

Its centre was in Etruria, north-west of Rome, where the Etruscans, organized in loosely federated city-states, profited by what they had learnt from Greek and oriental cultures to build up formidable military and industrial vigour. When this strength was at its height, their armies broke through southwards into Campania, where they founded (or refounded on the site of an earlier Italian township) the leading city of the entire fertile lowlands. This was Capua (S. Maria Capua Vetere), which lay 27 kilometres north of Neapolis and was the place that gave Campania its name.[6] Recent excavations on the site of Capua suggest that Etruscan penetration had begun by c. 650. Then, later on – apparently towards the end of the following century – they extended their domination over the greater part of the Campanian plain. This brought them into contact with the Greeks; and Cumae became the Etruscans' chief outlet to Greek commerce. In 524 BC and again in 474, they attacked the city, but were rebuffed. Nevertheless it seems probable that, during some period between those dates, the Etruscans controlled Pompeii. Or at all events they had trading contacts there, for fragments of Etruscan inscriptions have been noted on black vases found beneath the Temple of Apollo. It is also likely that they came to Herculaneum invading from Clusium and other inland Etruscan cities.

However, the rule of the Etruscans in the area did not survive their defeat in 474, and before long the vacuum was filled by the Samnites. These were tough hill-men – peasants and herdsmen – who came from fortified strong-points on the grey, landlocked, limestone plateau high up in the centre of the peninsula behind the plain. The language they spoke, a cousin of Latin, was called Oscan after earlier immigrants they supplanted in Samnium and Campania – the people who had lived at Pompeii and Capua before the Greeks and Etruscans arrived, and who had given Pompeii its name.[7] It was inevitable that the Samnites in their turn, as they began to exploit the strength of their own manpower and seek room for expansion, should covet these lowlands which were so much more fertile than their own fastnesses. Freed from the Etruscans – though their influence lingered on here and there – 'Oscan' Campania had formed itself into a separate federation of towns under the leadership of Capua, probably in 445 BC. But the Samnites descended upon Capua and took it by surprise in 423. Next, their covetous gaze turned to the Greek settlements along the coast. It was a good moment to attack them, since the mainland of Greece itself was too deeply immersed in the Peloponnesian War, between Athens on the one side and Sparta and Corinth on the other, to send any help. Consequently, the Greek colony of Cumae fell to the Samnites in 421–420, and its ancient important role was ended for ever. Very soon afterwards nearly all the other towns along the coast must have fallen into Samnite hands, Pompeii and Herculaneum among them; even Neapolis became a bicultural Greek and Samnite city. Soon, three Samnite Leagues were in existence – one in Samnium proper, one in Campania, and one in Lucania to the south-east. The Samnites largely imposed their own brand of the Oscan tongue upon these regions, but when, in the fourth century BC, they started to write it down, they employed for the purpose an adaptation of the Greek alphabet of Cumae. In addition, as they settled along the coast, they absorbed much of the Greek flair for business, which hitherto, in their former Samnite home country, had remained beyond their grasp.

Pompeii had thus become part of the first political unification of Campania by an Italic people; and, with the possible exception of Capua, it is more generous than any other place with material about this mysterious epoch. Perhaps, like Stabiae and Herculaneum, it took its orders, to some extent, from the larger centre of Nuceria in the immediate hinterland. But Samnite-ruled towns were notable for a strong republican and

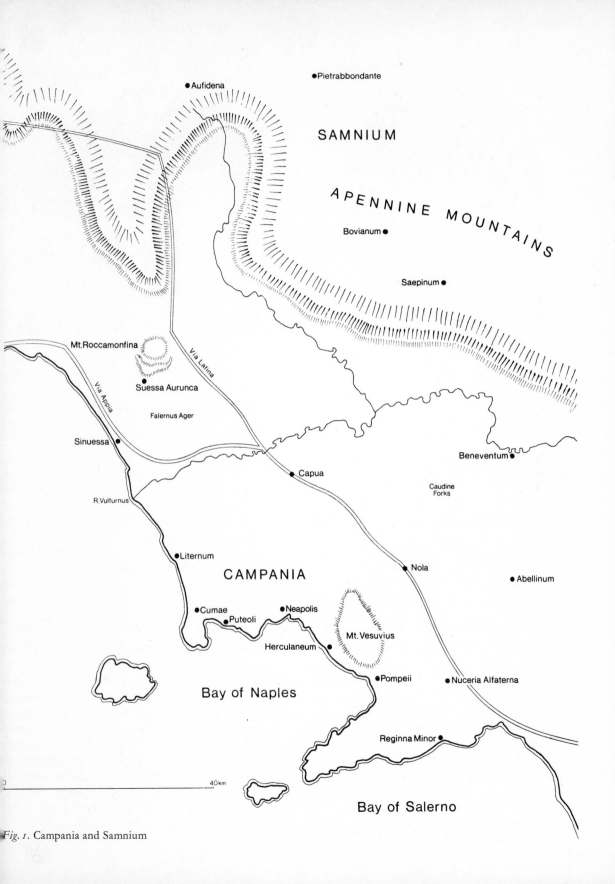

Fig. 1. Campania and Samnium

Above: Coin of the Italian rebels against Rome in the Social or Marsian War 91–87 BC. The head is inscribed ITALIA and the rebels are seen taking an oath. Pompeii and Herculaneum joined them and were overcome by Sulla

Opposite: Sulla: dictator and founder of the 'Colony of Venus' at Pompeii. A posthumous portrait, perhaps of *c* 59 BC

democratic tradition, and even the smaller places evidently retained or developed their own autonomous civic institutions. Though it is difficult to sift out what is truly Samnite from subsequent Roman accretions, it seems that the annually elected chief officials of Pompeii were not, initially, two in number (*duoviri*) as in Roman towns, but that there was a single functionary who presided, without equal colleagues, over an Assembly of the citizens of the town.[8]

But meanwhile the Romans, 208 kilometres to the north-west, were embarked on their long, grim, struggle for supremacy in Italy; and their road to Capua, the Via Latina, was already partially constructed by *c.* 370 (an alternative route, the Via Appia, had likewise been completed by the end of the century). Afraid of the Gauls who were penetrating the peninsula from the north, the Samnites, in *c.* 358–354, formed a defensive alliance with Rome. But then they and their Campanian relatives fell out, and the latter, afraid of further waves of Samnite invasion, took the fateful and ultimately fatal step of appealing

to Rome – or at least it was claimed by the Romans that such an appeal had been made. In the First Samnite War (in so far as it can be rescued from legend) the Romans seem to have entered Campania (*c.* 343). In the Second they captured Neapolis (327–326); then, in spite of a shattering defeat at the Caudine Forks in the interior (322), they landed at the mouth of the Sarnus, sacked Nuceria, and took Pompeii and presumably Herculaneum also (310–302). Even if the seizures of these towns may at first have been only temporary, by 300 Campania was wholly Roman, though Neapolis and Nuceria, now joined by road to Rome, were allowed nominal independence.

During the great invasion of Italy by Hannibal and the Carthaginians (218–204 BC), Capua revolted to the invader and paid the penalty (211), but Neapolis repulsed Hannibal, and Nuceria and Pompeii likewise apparently remained loyal to Rome. The Campanian cities profited greatly from the expansion of Roman power in the second century BC. Then in 91 BC, when the Italians, in their effort to obtain equal privileges, rebelled against the Romans in the Social or Marsian War, Nuceria again remained loyal, but Pompeii, Herculaneum and Stabiae joined the rebels.[9] Sulla, the future Roman dictator, retook and utterly destroyed Stabiae, which lost its lands to Nuceria and was restricted to a future as a spa. Herculaneum fell too. At Pompeii there are holes in the town-walls which bear witness to a siege, since they were caused by stones shot by siege-artillery *(ballistae)*. Lead missiles

the civil war that accompanied Sulla's return, the inhabitants of its rather overwhelming neighbour Neapolis were treacherously massacred.[13] In 73 BC Spartacus, leading a revolt of gladiators, offered a serious threat to the cities of Vesuvius, defeating Roman armies on the slopes of the mountain and again near Herculaneum. But finally he left the area, and his rebellion was crushed.

Thereafter not very much happened at these towns until their life came to an end. Augustus (31 BC–AD 14) left his mark on both places, just as he did on most others. Distinguished residents came and went. Later, in AD 59, there was a serious riot in the amphitheatre of Pompeii, between Pompeians and Nucerians, as a result of which the arena was closed for ten years, though the full period of closure may not have been enforced. But then in 62 came an earthquake,[14] and in 79 the fatal eruption, and of these something more must now be said.

have also been found outside the Herculaneum Gate, and inscriptions written in Oscan have been interpreted as signposts or duty rosters for the defending garrison. However, if the Oscan language still survived, it is scarcely likely to have continued in use much longer. For the siege almost certainly ended in capture by Sulla – whose name is found scratched on the plaster of a tower.[10] Then, at the end of the war, like the rest of Italy, Pompeii received the Roman franchise; and after Sulla had gone to the east, fought his campaigns there, and returned, the town was allotted its future role by the injection of a large draft of Roman settlers and the consequent conversion of the place into one of Sulla's self-governing 'colonies', known as the Colony of Venus (80 BC).

As befitted a region of which the dictator was particularly fond – he had a magnificent villa built for himself at Puteoli, where he died – he gave the colony his own nephew Publius Sulla as commissioner and 'patron', and it became a signal example of the building activity at which he excelled. It seems possible that the small-holdings which had to be found for the new settlers were largely carved out of lands taken not from Pompeians but from the people of ruined Stabiae,[11] although Cicero, in spite of this, records violent ill-will between the old citizens of Pompeii and the new colonists.[12] Herculaneum, too, had become a citizen-community like other Italian towns, but without new settlers; it may well, fortuitously, have gained a measure of independence when, during

Silver *Denarius* of Augustus, who left his mark on Pompeii and Herculaneum. Pompeii has a Temple of the Augustan Fortune, and there were Priests of the Divine Augustus at both towns. This coin shows his portrait and the effigy of his patron god Apollo of Actium

2. Vesuvius

The summit of Vesuvius is less than ten kilometres from Pompeii and less than seven from Herculaneum. The mountain belongs to a great chain of volcanoes – active, dormant or apparently extinct – stretching all the way from southern Tuscany down to Sicily and the adjoining Liparaean islands (Lipari), which were otherwise known, in ancient times, as Aeolian or Vulcanian. Mount Roccamonfina, north-west of Capua, has been silent for a very long time. The volcanoes still active today, or in recent years, are Vesuvius, Etna (Aetna) in Sicily, and Stromboli (Strongyle) in the Liparaean group. Vulcano (Thermessa Vulcani), another Liparaean island, was in eruption as short a time ago as 1890, and seven years earlier Mount Epomeo on Ischia erupted and destroyed a neighbouring town.

That island, known to the ancients as Pithecussae and Aenaria, lies off the north-western extremity of the Bay of Naples. Opposite to it on the mainland, behind Pozzuoli (Puteoli), extends the volcanic region known as the Phlegraean Fields (Campi Flegrei). It contains thirteen low craters, some filled with water, and there is an abundance of hot, bubbling springs and scalding blasts of steam. The eruptive activity of this very fertile region is apparently defunct – it is technically known as a 'volcanic wreck' – but on the very day on which these words are being written the newspapers have reported considerable anxiety because the gradual process of 'bradyseism', slow-motion volcanic earthquake, has recently and ominously raised the level of the Phlegraean mainland: the ground on which Pozzuoli itself is built has risen more than three-

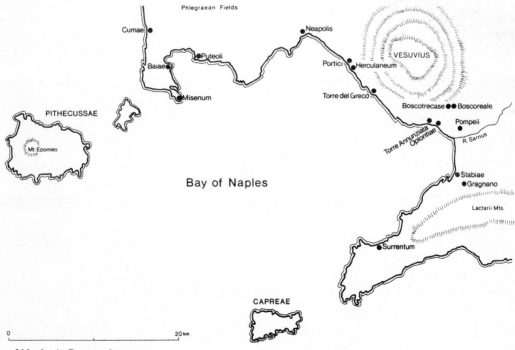

Fig. 2. The Bay of Naples in Roman times

quarters of a metre during the last six months. Simultaneously the coast-line of Ischia has sunk; and a series of minor earth tremors have been felt.

Far beneath the earth, Ischia's Mount Epomeo, the Phlegraean Fields, and Mount Vesuvius may share a common reservoir of seething molten matter. The volcanoes of the area could be in secret alliance.

For in Campania two fissures in the earth's crust meet, fuse and cross, and the craters of the area bear witness to this explosive situation. Conspicuous among them is Vesuvius, twelve kilometres south-east of Naples: the only active volcano on the European continent. The mountain stands up from the Campanian plain in isolation. Varying in maximum height around 1,200 metres – the height changes after each successive eruption – it comprises two peaks, Monte Vesuvio and Monte Somma. Monte Vesuvio contains the active crater, but far more ancient is the long extinct Monte Somma. Its original circle survives for about half the eleven kilometres of its circumference, partially encompassing the present cone of Monte Vesuvio. Beneath this lofty cliff long slopes descend to the plain.

The geographer Strabo, writing about the mountain early in the first century AD, had never heard of any eruptions throughout the whole course of past history, but he noted the fire-eaten appearance of the rocks and rightly detected volcanic origin.[1] The summit, he saw, was a wide, flat, sterile depression, with cliff walls.

When Spartacus led his rebellion of gladiators, he had established himself and his men in this crater, from which they later escaped by descending through unguarded cracks in its rim. They got down on twisted ropes of vine-branches, for Vesuvius (or Vesevus as people sometimes called it) no longer, as in earlier days, consisted of a dense forest famous for wild boars, but was covered all over with smiling vineyards. Virgil mentions these vines upon the slopes, as well as olives and good plough-land and grazing.[2] A painting which has survived from the House of the Centenary at Pompeii presumably indicates the approximate appearance of the mountain in the mid-first century AD, with vines growing up to a high level. This and two other paintings, now destroyed but copied before their destruction,[3] seem to show clearly enough that there was only one peak at the time (Monte Somma), not the two which exist today.

On 5 February AD 62,[4] a brilliantly sunny day, the region was convulsed by a serious earthquake. Damage was reported at Nuceria, and at Neapolis

Below: Reliefs in the shrine of the household gods in the House of Lucius Caecilius Jucundus at Pompeii, showing the earthquake of AD 62
Opposite: View of Vesuvius from the west, on a painting from the *lararium* of the House of the Centenary, Pompeii. The mountain is shown with a single cone and vegetation right up to the top. The figure is Dionysus (Bacchus) and the snake represents the household gods. Naples Museum

some buildings collapsed, but the destruction was much worse at Herculaneum, which suffered almost complete ruin, and at Pompeii, where the devastation was equally severe.

The heaving of the ground and reeling and crashing of statues, arches, columns and façades is shown naively but graphically on two reliefs which the Pompeian banker Lucius Caecilius Jucundus put up on the private shrine (lararium) of his house, perhaps in order to commemorate his own escape. The philosopher Seneca, who in his youth had written a study of earthquakes, gives a brief but interesting description of the upheaval of AD 62, mentioning that a whole flock of six hundred sheep was killed by the fumes.[5] Temples were destroyed, a large reservoir gave way, country mansions had to be abandoned, and a number of people went mad. But the towns were so prosperous and resilient that reconstruction rapidly went ahead.

However, the earthquake was ominous for the future, because it represented an abortive attempt by Vesuvius to blast out an open vent. Seventeen years later, on 24 August AD 79, the barrier was penetrated, and the mountain burst into eruption.[6]

For some days the festival of the divine Augustus had been in progress. In the capital, on the previous day, by a fitting and sinister coincidence, the annual festival of Vulcan had been celebrated; and 24 August was also the yearly occasion of an obscure rite, designed to give free egress to the inhabitants of the underworld. At Pompeii and the neighbouring towns there had been earthquake tremors for four days, and the springs had dried up because of a steep rise in pressure in the subterranean passages of the mountain. Then came the explosion.

A remarkable description of the disaster has survived. We owe it to the younger Pliny, who was at Misenum, beside the north-western extremity of the Bay of Naples. He was in the house of his uncle, the elder Pliny, historian, natural scientist and encyclopedic man of learning, who also happened to be commander of the Misenum naval base. Afterwards, another and greater historian, Tacitus, asked the younger Pliny to let him know what had happened; and this is what he reported.

My uncle was stationed at Misenum in active command of the fleet. On 24 August, in the early afternoon, my mother drew his attention to a cloud of unusual size and appearance. He had been out in the sun, had taken a cold bath, and lunched while lying down, and was then working at his books. He called for his shoes and climbed up to a place which would give him the best view of the phenomenon. It was not clear at that distance from which mountain the cloud was rising (it was afterwards known to be Vesuvius). Its general appearance can best be expressed as being like an umbrella pine, for it rose to a great height on a sort of trunk and then split off into branches, I imagine because it was thrust upwards by the first blast and then left unsupported as the pressure subsided, or else it was borne down by its own weight so that it spread out and gradually dispersed. In places it looked white, elsewhere blotched and dirty, according to the amount of soil and ashes it carried with it. My uncle's scholarly acumen saw at once that it was important enough for a closer inspection, and he ordered a boat to be made ready, telling me I could come with him if I wished. I replied that I preferred to go on with my studies, and as it happened he had himself given me some writing to do.

As he was leaving the house he was handed a message from Rectina, wife of Cascus whose house was at the foot of the mountain, so that escape was impossible except by boat. She was terrified by the danger threatening her and implored him to rescue her from her fate. He changed his plans, and what he had begun in a spirit of enquiry he completed as a hero. He gave orders for the warships to be launched and went on board himself with the intention of bringing help to many more people besides Rectina, for this lovely stretch of coast was thickly populated.

He hurried to the place which everyone else was hastily leaving, steering his course straight for the danger zone. He was entirely fearless, describing each new movement and phase of the portent to be noted down exactly as he observed them. Ashes were already falling, hotter and thicker as the ships drew near, followed by bits of pumice and blackened stones, charred and cracked by the flames: then suddenly they were in shallow water, and the shore was blocked by the debris from the mountain. For a moment my uncle wondered whether to turn back, but when the helmsman advised this he refused, telling him that Fortune stood by the courageous and they must make for Pomponianus at Stabiae. He was cut off there by the breadth of the bay (for the shore gradually curves round a basin

Cast of a man's head, with his mouth partly covered. From the Villa la Pisanella, Boscoreale. Pompeii Museum

filled by the sea) so that he was not as yet in danger, though it was clear that this would come nearer as it spread. Pomponianus had therefore already put his belongings on board ship, intending to escape if the contrary wind fell. This wind was of course full in my uncle's favour, and he was able to bring his ship in. He embraced his terrified friend, cheered and encouraged him, and thinking he could calm his fears by showing his own composure, gave orders that he was to be carried to the bathroom. After his bath he lay down and dined; he was quite cheerful, or at any rate he pretended he was, which was no less courageous.

Meanwhile on Mount Vesuvius broad sheets of fire and leaping flames blazed at several points, their bright glare emphasized by the darkness of night. My uncle tried to allay the fears of his companions by repeatedly declaring that these were nothing but bonfires left by the peasants in their terror, or else empty houses on fire in the districts they had abandoned.

Then he went to rest and certainly slept, for as he was a stout man his breathing was rather loud and heavy and could be heard by people coming and going outside his door. By this time the courtyard giving access to his room was full of ashes mixed with pumice-stones, so that its level had risen, and if he had stayed in the room any longer he would never have got out. He was wakened, came out and joined Pomponianus and the rest of the household who had sat up all night. They debated whether to stay indoors or take their chance in the open, for the buildings were now shaking with violent shocks, and seemed to be swaying to and fro as if they were torn from their foundations. Outside, on the other hand, there was the danger of falling pumice-stones, even though these were light and porous; however, after comparing the risks they chose the latter. In my uncle's case one reason outweighed the other, but for the others it was a choice of fears. As a protection against falling objects they put pillows on their heads tied down with cloths.

Elsewhere there was daylight by this time, but they were still in darkness, blacker and denser than any ordinary night, which they relieved by lighting torches and various kinds of lamps. My uncle decided to go down to the shore and investigate on the spot the possibility of any escape by sea, but he found the waves still wild and dangerous. A sheet was spread on the ground for him to lie down, and he repeatedly asked for cold water to drink. Then the flames and smell of sulphur which gave warning of the approaching fire drove the others to take flight and roused him to stand up. He stood leaning on two slaves and then suddenly collapsed, I imagine because the dense fumes choked his breathing by blocking his windpipe which was constitutionally weak and narrow and often inflamed.

When daylight returned on the 26th – two days after the last day he had been seen – his body was found intact and uninjured, still fully clothed and looking more like sleep than death.[7]

We do not know what use Tacitus made of this unique letter, for the portion of his *Histories* relating to the events of AD 79 has not survived. But the elder

A muleteer who died with his back to the wall of the athletics school (Palaestra). His mule was found nearby. Pompeii Museum

Pliny, by being present on this occasion, had supplemented his earlier attempts to write history by making it instead, and his nephew has given us the oldest surviving realistic description in western literature of a major natural disaster.

The admiral probably received the letter from his woman friend at about 2 p.m., though the younger Pliny is careful to explain that this was not the only reason why his uncle took the imperial fleet out. The message, which perhaps took two or three hours to reach him, had been written soon after the eruption started. Its first manifestation, which the Plinies neither witnessed nor apparently heard, had consisted of a tremendous noise, the bellowing of the mountain as it split. Two ancient writers refer to this phenomenon,[8] which is also confirmed by accounts of the eruption of 1872. The detonation was caused when the force of the internal gases demanding liberation caused the whole of Vesuvius to burst apart.

Opening up a new crater the volcano began to vomit red-hot boulders, large and small, and they were hurled up many thousands of metres high into the air. Then followed a continuous rushing upward blast of friction-pounded stones, cinders, ashes and dust, which first blotted out the light of the sun and eventually rained down on the surrounding countryside. The cloud, compared by Pliny to an umbrella pine, is a well-known accompaniment of volcanic activity. The electrical storms, 'broad sheets of fire and leaping lights', are quite frequent features of steam and ash eruptions; they were noted again over Vesuvius in 1779. During the catastrophe of 79, excavations have shown that a number of places were struck by this lightning. There were also lethal fumes, to which the corpulent elder Pliny succumbed. Nor was he the only person to die from this cause, for the contorted positions of many of those who perished at Pompeii testify to the deadly force of these asphyxiating agents, which at first, it has been concluded, were largely sulphurous, and were soon followed by gases impregnated with hydrochloric acid and other chlorides.

Pliny says nothing about the overwhelming of Pompeii, and no literary record of this aspect of the disaster exists. By the time his uncle had reached Stabiae, at about 4 p.m., Pompeii had already been buried for several hours, for when Vesuvius exploded, most of the contents poured forth by the mountain had settled in and around Pompeian territory. They fell in two successive layers, the first consisting of fragments of pumice stone which piled up to a height of between two and three metres above the ground, while the second layer, composed of ash, rose to a further two and a half metres.

A visitor to the area in our own century, Norman Douglas, had a dream about the eruption, in which he saw a torrent of warm and suffocating snow falling quietly, steadily, thickly from a black sky. But, during the centuries that have elapsed since the disaster, this snowy ash has been overlaid by a further two metres of solid fertile earth, so that when the excavators started work, Pompeii was hidden more than six metres beneath the surface.

The covering deposited by Vesuvius has formed such an effective preservative that when the Temple of Isis was discovered, eggs and fish were still to be seen on its dining-room table, and in the bakery of Modestus eighty-one carbonized loaves were still in the oven; put in only a few seconds earlier, they had been left with the iron door closed. In the kitchen of the House of the Vettii, pots standing on tripods still contained meat bones. In the Macellum, the market in the Forum, there was fruit in its glass containers.

The fate of Herculaneum was very different. The hail of pumice and ashes which overwhelmed Pompeii did not come its way at all. But what descended instead was mud. For, in addition to the rain of solid projectiles, the mountain also belched forth a torrent of steam escaping at a heat of 2000° Fahrenheit (930° Centigrade). Condensing and mingling with seawater spray, this steam produced scorching local downpours, which churned up the lava surface of the mountain into a boiling mass. This 'mud-lava', as it is called (in contrast to 'fire-lava', expelled from the crater itself, which has occurred in later eruptions), formed a torrid, treacly river which poured down the deep ravines and obliterated Herculaneum, on the flanks of the mountain, to a depth of between fifteen and eighteen metres.

Gradually, the mass cooled, and solidified to the consistency of rock. It is an alarming experience (now denied to the public without special permission) to go right down into the dank, dripping, bone-chilling depths of the Theatre of Herculaneum, which was tunnelled by eighteenth-century diggers but is still buried deep in the earth. Giacomo Leopardi was thinking of this place when he wrote of Topaia, the subterranean capital of the Mouse State which could only be visited with the aid of torches; and Charles

Above: The swimming pool of the sports ground at Herculaneum, rediscovered under the mass of volcanic mud that covered the town. The point where the serpent fountain stands was originally the centre of a great colonnaded court

Opposite: A shop front in the main street of Herculaneum. Some of the original timber has been preserved. The brick was originally covered with coloured stucco

Dickens was 'perplexed by great walls of monstrous thickness, making the whole place a disordered dream'.

The hot mud moved on Herculaneum with a curious mixture of irresistible violence and gentle delicacy. Mud-flows only a metre high can move boulders weighing a hundred thousand kilos for hundreds of metres down gradients of a mere five degrees; and at Herculaneum fragments of the same piece of sculpture have been found at intervals along a single street. The buildings of the town were bull-dozed into ruin, and yet the mud preserved many things even better than the ash of Pompeii. In its slow but inexorable procession, the torrid ooze filled rooms without disturbing the position of the cradle in the nursery, or the pots on the kitchen stove. Cooling, it scorched cloth and papyrus; but it did not destroy them. Nor did it pulverize wood. It only carbonized it, so that the material, though organically transformed, has remained in existence, like a pole in a bog of peat. And so beams, stairs, furniture, a wooden clothes press, a cupboard, a little household shrine with gods

still inside, a temporary scaffold supporting a sagging roof, all were saved.

Indeed, even egg-shells remained intact – as at Pompeii – in this same carbonized condition, within a kitchen cupboard, and again on a dining-room table in the House of the Relief of Telephus, where they were found with the rest of the lunch – bread, salad, cakes and fruit – that was being served when the catastrophe struck. On the counter of the green-grocer Aulus Fuferus the beans and grain had not been destroyed. In the shop of the Drinking Priapus there were large, almost full jars of nuts under the counter, with a few set out as samples. Near the Forum a shipment of valuable glassware had recently arrived in a special case packed with straw; the first layer of the packing had just been torn away. The remains of matting that formed the covering of a bed also escaped destruction. So did pieces of rope and fishermen's nets, and even wax tablets. Such things continued to exist for all those hundreds of years, far below the new ground-level the eruption had so ruthlessly clapped down on top of them.

Yet in Herculaneum relatively few dead men and women have come to light, because the mud-lava flowed slowly enough for most of the inhabitants to be able to get out of the town – though they may not always have got much further. Inside the place itself, not more than twenty or thirty skeletons have been found. Two were discovered seven and half metres above the level of the ancient street; they had been forced upwards in the half-liquid mass. At a gem-cutter's shop a sick boy was left lying on an elegantly veneered bed, and beside him was the chicken that had been prepared for his lunch. In the College of the Priests of Augustus a man in an expensively furnished room failed to make his escape.

At Pompeii, on the other hand, which was over-whelmed so much more precipitately by hot pumice and ash, there are many signs of people who were caught by surprise, and had to take what hasty measures they could. In the House of the Philosopher, there was evidently no time to rescue the silver cups that had been laid at the guests' places. But in the House of Pansa a valuable piece of sculpture, rep-resenting Bacchus and a satyr, was placed for safety in a copper kettle in the garden. In the House of the Ephebe, on the other hand, a statue was removed from the garden to the partially covered atrium, where it was covered with a cloth, and heavy candlesticks

were removed from its hands. In the Villa of Publius Fannius Sinistor (or Lucius Herennius Florus) at Boscoreale (just north of Pompeii) a slave carried a sack full of valuable silver plates to a room containing an oil-press, where he dumped his burden in the well.

The slave was one of those who died. In and around Pompeii something like 2,000 people perished – about one-tenth of the population – in addition to the large numbers who must have vanished without trace in the surrounding countryside. In 1771 a sensation was created by the discovery in the Villa of Diomede, just outside the town, of a young girl's skeleton, with the shape of her bosom preserved by hardened sand. This 'magnifique sein de femme' prompted Gautier's novel Arria Marcella (1852). But then in 1864 Giuseppe Fiorelli, who was in charge of the excavations, discovered an almost perfect way of recapturing the appearance of the dead. He found that in most cases the ash had hardened so closely around the corpses that, when they subsequently decomposed, their exact contour was still preserved round the hollow

space. He therefore formed the idea of forcibly blowing into this hollow a special solution of liquid plaster, which then solidified and exactly reproduced the shape of the body. The result is astonishing. Even the outlines of clothes are preserved; it can be noted that a beggar outside the Nucerian Gate, carrying a sack for alms, was wearing good quality sandals – perhaps from public charity. On other bodies reconstructed in this way, even the shape of their pubic hair can be detected, and the fact that it was shaved in semi-circular form, as on certain statues. And the tormented facial expressions are all too clear.

'The great aim of archaeology,' said Philippe Diolé, 'is to restore the warmth and truth of life to dead objects.' Here there is hardly warmth, but a very high, a painful, degree of truth. That, apart from ghoulish gloating, must be the answer to the impassioned query of one visitor, Edward Hutton: 'Why should our curiosity demand so horrible an outrage as this?' In 1906 Jung pointed out to Freud the psychological implications of a recent book, Gradiva by Wilhelm

Jensen, whose fetishistic treatment of parts of the body was clearly inspired by the dead men and women whose forms he had seen at Pompeii.

The first deaths in the town were caused when pieces of lava, released by the initial explosion, crashed down from an enormous height. Next, as people hid or ran about in a panic, they were suffocated by ash, asphyxiated by fumes, or obliterated by falling columns and masonry. Many found that the places where they had taken cover proved to be fatal traps. Others were trampled to death in the pitch blackness, which was broken only by lethal electric flashes.

In the House of Menander the slaves seem to have decided to flee upstairs and get out by the window or roof. But they were borne down by pumice and ashes; and ten of them died between the stairs and the door, including their leader with his bronze lantern. One of the party had hacked a hole in the wall of the room, but to no purpose. Meanwhile the doorkeeper had retired to his office by the entrance, carrying his master's seal and a purse, which contained two coins of gold, ninety of silver and thirteen of brass and copper. He took his little girl with him, and covered himself and her with cushions and pillows; and that is how death overtook them. In the House of the Cryptoporticus a mother with her small daughter in her arms took refuge in an underground room, and

Above: House of Menander, Pompeii. The hole pierced in the wall by a member of the household who was taking refuge from the eruption
Opposite: The beggar struck down outside the Nucerian Gate, Pompeii. He had received good sandals, perhaps from public charity, and was found holding a sack containing alms
Left: Found in the House of Menander, Pompeii

subsequently got out through a skylight into the garden; but there she was struck down. In a house on the Via Stabiana they closed the atrium with an iron shutter, but in vain because all the twelve people inside perished of suffocation. The women who succumbed in the House of Pansa, and in the recently excavated House of Marcius Fabius Rufus, were wearing golden ear pendants, necklaces and rings. Outside the House of Sallust, the mistress of the mansion and her three maids all lay dead in the ash. Strewn around the lady were her jewellery, her money, and a silver mirror: valuables which she had evidently taken too long to collect. In the House of Publius Paquius Proculus, when the upper storey crumbled on top of a ground-floor room, seven children were buried in the debris.

When the Temple of Isis was endangered or began to collapse, the priests set out with the temple treasure. One of their number, carrying a linen bag full of gold coins, fell at the corner of the Via dell'Abbondanza, and did not rise again. The others moved on to the Triangular Forum, where two were killed by its crashing columns, and their costly sacred emblems were scattered. The survivors took refuge in a house, but found they were trapped. One of them broke through two walls with an axe. But then he collapsed, with the weapon still in his hand.

At a tavern in the Via di Nola, gladiators abandoned their half-finished drinks and fled for their lives, leaving behind a collection of trumpets – the instruments they used to make announcements in the arena.

Cast of a young woman who was a victim of Vesuvius. Pompeii Museum

Perhaps they got away. If so, they were more fortunate than over sixty of their colleagues who perished in the Gladiators' Barracks. The dead men included two who had been locked up in a prison cell with manacled wrists; no one had time to think of them now. Much prurient speculation has been aroused by the presence in the barracks of a richly dressed woman. She died with the gladiators she was visiting.

Not far from the Barracks, a slave was found near a horse loaded with stuffs and clothing and valuables. But elsewhere the bodies of beasts of burden are hardly ever found, because the people who were hastening away from the town mobilized them all. In front of the tradesmen's entrance of the House of Menander a cart packed with wine-jars was left behind. Everything was ready for departure, but at the last moment the animals had been hastily unharnessed and mounted instead.

Dogs were not always so fortunate. One has been reconstructed by Fiorelli's plaster technique, with macabre completeness. It was in the atrium of the House of Vesonius Primus, tethered to a chain. As the ash rained down through the opening in the ceiling and piled up all around, the animal climbed as high as its chain would allow, and then, contorted in agony, died. In the House of the Vestals another dog perished, beside a man. But after the man expired (or so it is to be hoped), the dog, as it got hungry, gnawed its master's body, for his bones were found to bear the marks of its teeth.

Cast of a dog from the House of Vesonius Primus. It died struggling with its chain. Pompeii Museum

Outside the walls the casualties were just as bad, or worse. Near the Nola Gate a man had climbed a tree. In the Villa of the Mysteries, outside the Herculaneum Gate, a door-keeper died in his office (wearing an iron ring with a chalcedony seal), a girl fell at the entrance, and three women wearing fine jewels and gold met their deaths in an upper room, including a young girl clutching a little bronze mirror. In the neighbouring Villa of Diomede eighteen people were found dead in the cellar, among them two boys locked in each other's arms. Near the secondary entrance of the same mansion lay its owner, holding a silver key; and with him was his steward, with a store of money and other possessions. In a villa at Boscoreale, the owner's wife and a companion took refuge in the courtyard that contained the presses, protecting their faces with cloaks; but they did so in vain. At a house with a wine business in the Street of Tombs, thirty-four of the occupants went down to the vault, and prepared themselves for a long stay by taking bread, fruit and a goat. But neither they nor their goat ever came up

A gold necklace from Pompeii; many such pieces of jewellery were found on women who died in the eruption. Naples Museum

again. Another goat, and its master, succumbed nearby, out in the open. The animal was being dragged along by the halter, since it was probably its owner's most valuable possession.

These casualties occurred outside the northern walls of Pompeii, close beneath the mountain. But many fugitives must rather have turned in the opposite direction, and crowded out of the southern gates in the direction of the coast. A lot of them, however, were unlucky, for many skeletons, surrounded by gold and silver and all kinds of jewellery, were found south of the town, at the place where the river Sarnus may in those days have entered the bay. For in addition to the perils by land, bridges across the stream and moles at the harbour had no doubt been shattered, and many ships and boats must have been sunk or immobilized by the terrifying rain of objects from the sky. Escape was also blocked by the extreme heat and turbulence of the waves and by the blasts of wind which, as Pliny tells us, were blowing violently off the sea.

Pompeii and Herculaneum were not the only towns destroyed by the eruption. Stabiae, five kilometres south of Pompeii, was likewise obliterated, as the large ruined villas in the neighbourhood confirm (the town itself has vanished). At the time of the eruption the elder Pliny realized that Stabiae was not a safe place to land, and it was there, on the beach, that he met his death as we have seen. Those who were with him when he collapsed got away none too soon, leaving his body to be recovered later.

As Vesuvius rained down pumice and ash over seventeen kilometres of the countryside, six other towns or villages were also blotted out. Their names were Oplontiae (or Oplontis), Taurania, Tora, Sora, Cossa and Leucopetra. Oplontiae was on the coast between Pompeii and Herculaneum, and nearer the former. At all those places, when the process of locating them is complete, rich discoveries lie in store for future excavators.

Since, as Pliny tells us, the gale was blowing into Stabiae off the sea, it was blowing away from Neapolis, which escaped with nothing worse than earth tremors, although, when the direction of the wind later changed, a small and harmless blanket of ash descended on the city. As for Misenum at the far end of the bay, twenty-six kilometres from the mountain, another of the young man's letters to Tacitus describes how things went there.

The buildings around us were tottering . . . The carriages we had ordered to be brought out began to run in different directions though the ground was quite level, and would not remain stationary even when wedged with stones. We also saw the sea sucked away and apparently forced back by the earthquake . . . quantities of sea creatures were left stranded on dry land. On the landward side a fearful black cloud was rent by forked and quivering bursts of flame, and parted to reveal great tongues of fire, like flashes of lightning magnified in size . . . Then ashes began to fall again, this time in heavy showers.[9]

At last the darkness thinned into a drifting column of smoke – that inverted 'L', carried off at a sharp angle, which has often been seen after modern eruptions. It was likely, as Goethe noted, that this smoke, which was composed largely of stones and ashes, drifted for a long time like clouds. The historian Dio Cassius, a century and a half after the eruption, read that the sun was darkened at Rome; and the wind carried fine ash as far as the coasts of north Africa and the Levant.

Except for the eruption of Mount Krakatoa in Indonesia in 1883, and perhaps the explosion of Mount Pelée on Martinique and Mount Soufrière (Saint Vincent) in 1902, this was the greatest catastrophe inflicted by any volcano within historical memory, though, before the beginning of recorded history – in the second millennium BC – the outburst of Thera (Santorin) in the Aegean appears to have been on an even larger scale. It may well have been at this time, in AD 79, that Vesuvius started to bifurcate, at just over half its height, into two peaks: the ancient Monte Somma – with part of its south wall blown away – and the new, active cone of Monte Vesuvio, separated from it by the Atrio del Cavallo, a sickle-shaped ravine in the old crater floor.

Titus, who had become emperor only a month before the disaster, took whatever measures he could to help the homeless. He arranged for a commission of senators to be appointed by lot to look after the ruined district; he assigned the property of those victims who had died intestate to purposes of relief, and he gave privileges to towns which offered assistance to the refugees. When they fled from the eruption, they had scattered to Nola (nineteen kilometres inland), Neapolis, Surrentum (Sorrento) at the southern end of the bay, and Capua. Now the territory of abandoned Pompeii was joined on to Nola; and the survivors from Herculaneum were permitted to attach the name of their vanished town to the quarter allotted to them at Neapolis. Titus's commissioners were instructed to study the situation and plan rebuilding on the old sites.[10] But this was never done. In the region of Pompeii, henceforward, there were only a few wine-growers' huts, the 'Campo Pompeiano' which eventually grew into the modern town. At Herculaneum, which was resettled rather more quickly, the new inhabitants formed the village that has now become Resina. Stabiae alone, near the fringe of the stricken area, managed to recover on a considerable scale, taking over the trade-routes which had previously belonged to Pompeii. Today, under the name of Castellamare di Stabia, it is a town of over 70,000 inhabitants.

Since then, Vesuvius has erupted on seventy further occasions. According to Dio Cassius the phenomenon

Coin of Titus (AD 79–81), who had become sole emperor one month before the eruption of Vesuvius, and ordered measures of relief for its survivors. The design shown here, inscribed I V D (aea) C A P (ta), refers to his suppression of the revolt of the Jews, who regarded the eruption as divine retribution

in AD 202, which lasted for a week, was accompanied
by 'bellowings mighty enough to be heard even in
Capua'.[11] In 306 there was a recurrence: and there was
another in 471, preceded by three years of menacing
disturbances. The eruption in 513 was followed by a
further outburst twenty years later, from which we
have our first record of fire-lava streams pouring from
the crater, as opposed to the 'mud-lava' of 79. Then
came centuries of relative calm, broken by activity in
1306–8. After 1500 there were many years of absolute
quiescence, with the mountain cultivated up to the
cone, and the crater itself covered with trees; in the
seventeenth century the slopes were still thick with
forests and teeming with game.

But then on 16 December 1631, after six months of
earth tremors, the inhabitants of the region experienced
the second worst eruption there has ever been. While
Vesuvius, as an observer declared, 'sweated fire', lava
poured out from the crater and descended in seven
streams, covering the site of Herculaneum and
surging onwards to the sea. Nearly all the towns at
the foot of the mountain were destroyed, and large
numbers of people met their deaths; the total was
variously estimated at 3,000 and 18,000. The mountain
hurled stones a great distance into the sky, and the
cloud drifted as far as Taranto. The crater of Monte
Vesuvio enlarged itself nearly threefold, and the top
of the ancient Monte Somma was sawn off. 'In the
heart of this mountain,' concluded Emmanuele
Fonseca, Viceroy of Naples, 'is stored much evil.'

Since then there have been over twenty eruptions
more. Sometimes they have emitted lava and
sometimes only steam and dust and fragments of
stone. They are the subject of many a lurid painting
and drawing in the Museo Nazionale San Martino at
Naples and elsewhere. Towns on the coast, such as
Torre Annunziata beside Pompeii and Torre del
Greco near Herculaneum, have repeatedly been
covered or destroyed.

In 1707 an eruption lasted from May to August,
covering Naples with dense showers of ashes. Later
in the century, during his tenure as British Minister in
the city, Sir William Hamilton, who deserves to be
known for more than the sharing of his wife Emma
with Nelson, climbed to the summit no less than
sixty-eight times, and witnessed eruptions in 1767 and
again in 1794, when 'the sea-water was boiling as in a

Eighteenth-century print of Vesuvius in eruption. Resina
(Herculaneum) is seen bottom left

VESUVIUS MONS

Montis interioris
conspectus.

Mare

Mediter... ...raneum

cauldron'. On one occasion the mountain was docked of a substantial piece of its height, and the same thing happened again in June 1858.

The important eruption of 1872 was preceded by terrific thundering. Then stones and lava were thrown 1,300 metres up into the sky, clouds of ashes rose to twice that height, and streams of lava oozed for a distance of five kilometres, travelling at an average rate of 400 metres an hour. Between 1895 and 1899 there was a whole series of disturbances. Then the year 1906 witnessed one of the greatest eruptions on record, again changing the contours of the mountain, plunging Naples into darkness (the wind was blowing that way), and elevating the umbrella-pine cloud to a height of 4,500 and finally 9,000 metres.

Finally in 1944, after a long dormant period, came the most recent outburst of Vesuvius, precipitated by a collapse of the cone which had obstructed the crater's mouth. Continuing for twelve days, the eruption destroyed Cook's funicular railway, and toppled the dome of the church at Nocera Superiore. The day of 18 March, when this violent activity began, was calm and windless, and the ashes hovered in the air for hours before descending upon Pompeii. But they lay less than half a metre deep, and Herculaneum was not affected.

In the following month the main fissure closed, and closed it still is. Its cone, Monte Vesuvio, was last reported to be about 1,270 metres high, taller than the loftiest point (Punta del Nasone) of the great prehistoric crater of Monte Somma which half encircles it.

The foothills are still very fertile and densely populated. But the upper part of the mountain is now barren. Streaked by contorted, ropy, lunar heaps of volcanic material and littered by great, formless, grey

The cone of Vesuvius before the eruption of 1944 closed the crater

chunks, it is just a gigantic cinder heap, infernally sultry and torrid in summer. To the nineteenth-century visitor, Dean A.P. Stanley, the contrast between these bare and lurid tracts of desolation and the smiling lands below seemed aptly to symbolize the theological studies with which his contemporaries occupied themselves, profitable at times but often insupportably arid.

Other travellers applied a sharper and less specialized vision to this juxtaposition and conflict between the enhancement and demolition of life. Goethe, recollecting in later life his Italian journey of 1787, had seen Vesuvius as a peak of hell rising out of paradise. In 1836 Giacomo Leopardi, in his meditative, satirical poem *La Ginestra* (meaning the humble broom, which an eruption will later wipe out), envisaged the mountain as a perpetual threat to existence which is nonetheless perpetually regenerated in its shadow.

Nine years later Charles Dickens, too, noted 'the strange and melancholy sensation of seeing the Destroyed and the Destroyer making this quiet picture in the sun'.

And now, again, the scene may well arouse the same Manichaean instinct in ourselves. For the nuclear age in which we live, besides renewing our familiarity with umbrella clouds, means that the condition of our existence is truly and unceasingly Pompeian. Moreover the volcano itself is not yet domesticated, like, for example, Mount Edgcumbe in New Zealand, which provides steam to heat houses and make paper and plastics. Besides, one day Vesuvius will offer its own, by no means contemptible, brand of explosion again. Some say it bursts into activity, on an average, every seventeen years; others say every twenty-five. And since the last eruption the number of years that have passed is already twenty-seven.

Fig. 3. Pompeii

Villa of Mysteries

Villa of Diomede

Street of Tombs

Villa of Cicero

Railway stn.
V. Misteri
(Circumvesuviana)

Herculaneum Gate

Tower 1¹

Vesuvius Gate

H. of Vestals
H. of Surgeon

H. of Sallust

H. of Pansa

H. of Small Fountain
H. of Large Fountain
H. of Tragic Poet

Forum Baths

Via del Foro

H. of Faun

H. of Vettii

H. of Golden Cupids

H. of Silver Wedding

H. of Lucretius Fronto

H. of Vesonius Primus

Central Baths

H. of Centenary

T. of Fortuna Augusta

Bakery of Modestus

Inn of Asellina

Fullery of Verecundus

H. of Fabi

T. of Jupiter

Provision Market

Hotel of Sittius

Brothel

H. of Cryptc

T. of Lares
T. of Vespasian

Stabian Baths

H. of Casca Longus
Fullery of Stephanus

T. of Apollo

Forum

Building of Eumachia

Via dell' Abbondanza

H. of Citharist

Marine Gate

Museum

T. of Venus

Basilica

Hall of Duovin

Hall of Aediles

Town Council

Small Palaestra

Isis

T. of Jupiter Milichius

Triangular Forum

Large Theatre

Odeon

Villa of Marine Gate

Doric

Gladiatorial Barracks

3. The Towns and their Meeting Places

Pompeii covered about 64 hectares and its circumference measured three kilometres – about the average for an Italian town of the early empire. The population was probably about 20,000.

The place was of an irregular oval shape. Though opinions on the subject differ, it appears probable that the original nucleus was the low, flat part of the town

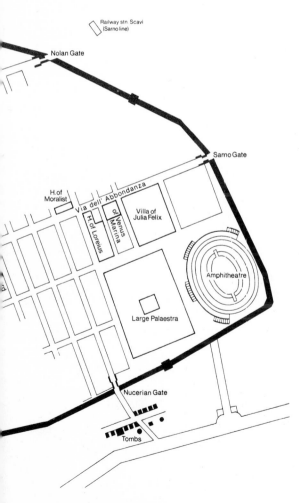

in the south-western corner (including the later Forum), and that in this district there was an irregularly planned, close-packed huddle of buildings, lying beneath a citadel on the southern spur (the Triangular Forum), where remains of an early Doric Temple have been found. Then in the late fifth century BC, shortly before or after the Samnite incursions, the inhabited zone was progressively enlarged by a series of rectilinear extensions. Town-planning of this orderly, geometric type was ultimately derived from the Greek architect and urban planner Hippodamus of Miletus, who designed a Pan-Hellenic foundation at Thurii (formerly Sybaris) in south-eastern Italy (443 BC). From there his ideas spread northwards into Campania, where Capua was famous for its broad layout.[1] But the Pompeian grid is much less precise than the norm of Hippodamus, not conforming with rigid rectangularity or uniformly fixed widths for house-blocks, though these are normally made squarish, averaging 59·50 metres each way. However, despite this lack of exactness, Pompeii, with the doubtful exception of Marzabotto near Bologna (Bononia), provides the earliest known systematic urban layout in Italy, representing an impressively high standard for this early date.

The next signs of really vigorous expansion hardly occur until the latter half of the second century BC, when the processes of development that took place recalled the evolution of contemporary Greek cities such as Delos in the Aegean. Early in the next century Sulla's colony at Pompeii received new and grander adornments; and then Augustus added his quota. But the architects, builders and designers enjoyed their greatest boom of all under Nero, as a result of the earthquake of 62 AD. For thereafter, during the last seventeen years of the town's life, they were called upon, not indeed to expand the area of Pompeii, but to rebuild all the numerous buildings the earthquake had damaged or destroyed. However, this took a long time. Even at private houses the reconstructors never finished their work, and the grand scheme for recreating the public buildings was in many cases scarcely begun before total obliteration descended in 79.

We cannot say much about the lay-out of the original little Pompeii; it may have been based on two roads intersecting at the northern end of the Forum. When the town reached its final dimensions, it was crossed by two main intersecting streets, the principal thoroughfare being the Via dell'Abbondanza, and the other the Via Stabiana. As is clear from these modern Italian names, which are habitually used to describe the streets, we are usually unaware of what they were called in ancient times; though the Via Stabiana is, in

this respect, an exception, since an inscription discovered at the Gate shows it was called the 'Via Pompeiana'.

It always surprises visitors to find how narrow most ancient streets were. At Pompeii they are 2·4, 3·6 or 4·5 metres wide, the widest of all measuring just over seven metres. (As will be seen, Herculaneum had a street that was much larger.) This narrowness provided some shade, and so did overhanging balconies. On the other hand the streets were not necessarily as dark at nights as has sometimes been supposed; a poster refers to a lamp-lighter *(lanternarius)*, and the good lighting which we know to have existed at cities such as Alexandria was probably not altogether absent at Pompeii. The Via Stabiana is

Model of the excavations at Pompeii. At the bottom, in the middle, beside the large theatre, is a Doric Temple of the sixth century BC, in the Triangular Forum which had perhaps been the earliest meeting-place of Pompeii. The oblong space to the extreme left is the Forum which subsequently became the town centre. Naples Museum

uneven, running down from north-west to south-east along the steepest of the prehistoric lava slopes. The Via dell'Abbondanza (running from north-east to south-west) is again crooked and irregular, and the intersection of these two main arteries is not at the right angles required by Greek urbanistic theory. Madame de Staël found that these cross-roads got on her nerves: 'It seems that one is waiting for someone, that the master is about to appear.'

Mark Twain, in his *Innocents Abroad* (1869), showed a great interest in the paving stones, products of Vesuvius itself which is 'the ever present genius of the scene'. But he was scandalized by the deep ruts. 'Have I not seen with my own eyes how ruts five and even ten inches deep were worn into the thick flagstones

by the chariot-wheels of generations of swindled taxpayers?' Except when a smoother limestone was occasionally used, the streets of Pompeii and Herculaneum were paved with slabs of a strong, grey Vesuvian lava which is still used for the same purpose in Naples; the wheel-ruts to which Mark Twain objected are deepest where the blocks came from near the surface of the quarries. On either side of the principal streets there were raised pavements or sidewalks; but as the streets contained running water and garbage, large stepping stones were placed to enable pedestrians to cross from one side to the other. They must have been highly obstructive to traffic. But axles of ancient waggons and carts were normally high enough to clear the stones,[2] and the draught

The Via Stabiana, seen from the north

Overleaf: The cross-roads of the Via Stabiana and Via degli Augustali, Pompeii

animals had more freedom of movement than their modern counterparts, since they were attached to their vehicles only by the yoke.

At many of the street intersections there are fountains, with sculptured headstones over rectangular stone troughs which are marked with the depressions slowly worn by the hands and buckets of passers-by. At Pompeii the fountains, as well as various buildings (including spacious public lavatories in the Forum and elsewhere), were fed with water by lead pipes running beneath the sidewalks from two huge cisterns, one at the Vesuvian Gate (high up in the town, so that the pipes could be placed at a downward angle), and the other near the Forum Baths. The relief in the House of Lucius Caecilius Jucundus which depicts the earthquake of AD 62 shows that the upheaval caused at least one of these reservoirs to be breached. Water came to the cisterns from the inland hills by an aqueduct which started from Serino near Avellino (the ancient Abellinum, twenty-six kilometres inland) and passed beside Vesuvius to the north, supplying Neapolis and Misenum; and then a branch was added to Pompeii, reaching the town at the Vesuvian gate. Before this, the place had depended on rain-water cisterns, augmented in due course by a considerable number of street wells, of which some penetrated through the prehistoric lava to springs thirty metres deep.

Herculaneum possessed a better drainage system than Pompeii. Its arrangements included a sizeable, expertly constructed underground sewer, and drains which ran beneath the roads and conveyed sewage and rain-water to the sea. These constructions prevented the streets from becoming waterlogged, and provided one reason why the stepping stones introduced for the pedestrians of Pompeii were not needed at Herculaneum. Another reason, which I shall come to later on, was the scarcity of vehicles.

The walls of Pompeii represent one of the most important systems of fortifications that have survived from any pre-Roman Italian town. There were at least four phases of construction. The first consisted of an earthwork, buttressed by wooden boards and crowned by a palisade. Then, in the middle of the fifth century BC, a facing of tufa (volcanic dust hardened by water into rock) and Sarnus limestone was added. It is impossible to tell whether the impulse was Greek, Etruscan or Samnite, but at all events the defences at this period consisted of two parallel walls – as at the Samnite town of Saepinum, but there the gap between the walls is only three metres wide, not six as here; at Aufidena (Alfidena) in the same country there were three circuits instead of two. At Pompeii the interspace between the two parts of the protective screen was filled with stones and earth. The inner wall, about twelve metres high, was some two metres taller than its external counterpart, which still backed on a sloping bank or earth-covered buttress (adjoining a moat) in the Italian fashion, in contrast to the Greek preference for vertical fortifications. There were loopholes for archers and slingers.

In the second century BC the defences were further strengthened, and finally, in about 100, twelve towers were added. Tower No. 11, which has been restored, shows that a square shape was preferred, contrary to the advice later given by the architect and military engineer Vitruvius, who suggested that corners should be avoided, since they made masonry liable to damage from missiles. As was mentioned in Chapter 1, the towers and walls bear marks and inscriptions relating to the military operations which brought Pompeii's independence to an end in 89 BC.

Tower No. 11 is one of three grouped closely together on a small, particularly vulnerable northwesterly sector of the wall, between the Vesuvius and Herculaneum Gates. Six further towers are distributed at points where they can reinforce other gates. Pompeii had seven entrances, five of which led to highways outside the town. Some of the gates, consisting of outer and inner openings separated by an unroofed court, date back to the second century BC. The oldest seems to be the Stabian Gate to the south, comprising a narrow passage under a single arch flanked by powerful bulwarks descending in a slope to an outer moat. Next towards the east is the Nucerian Gate (discovered in the 1950s), and towards the west stands the Marine Gate or Gate to the Sea.

A tower on the city-wall near the Vesuvian Gate, Pompeii

Too steep for vehicles, this consisted of a single barrel-vault containing two passage-ways – a ramp for pack-animals and a flight of steps for pedestrians. Then, to the north, came the Herculaneum Gate, of which we happen, for once, to know the ancient name: it was called the 'Porta Saliniensis', since it led to a village of salt-pan workers. This gateway had three openings, a central arch for vehicles and two side-passages for travellers on foot. Further towards the north come the Vesuvius, Nola and Sarnus Gates. The middle one of these, the Nola Gate, is the most impressive and formidable from a military point of view.

In due course, as defence became less important, this functional military style gave way to more complex structures such as the Herculaneum Gate. Moreover, there now began a tendency to add elaborate decorations, often including a statue of Minerva, protectress of traders. By this time the walls themselves hardly fulfilled a defensive purpose any more, and on either side of the Marine Gate large stretches of wall were knocked down altogether, to facilitate the construction of houses. This contravened a regulation which forbade building on strips just inside and outside the wall; and Vespasian (AD 69–79) sent a commissioner, Suedius Clemens, who enforced the latter part of the prohibition, though evidently not the former.

Just outside the walls lay large areas mainly given up to cemeteries, since burial and cremation (which became the more frequent, solemn, and elaborate rite of the two) were forbidden inside the town, just as they were forbidden inside Rome itself by the ancient

Opposite: Looking into Pompeii through the Nucerian Gate. Vesuvius is in the background
Below: Leaving Pompeii by the Herculaneum Gate

Overleaf: The Street of the Tombs (Via dei Sepolcri) outside the Herculaneum Gate, Pompeii. On the right is the tomb of Marcus Umbricius Scaurus, a fish sauce merchant

The cemetery outside the Nucerian Gate, Pompeii. The
second tomb from the left is that of Lucius Cellius,
a senior army officer (*tribunus militum*)

Law of the Twelve Tables. The two principal
cemeteries extended outside the Herculaneum and
Nuceria Gates, where long stretches of road, one
leading out of town and the other running parallel to
the wall, show an uninterrupted succession of tombs.[3]
Their exteriors, rectangular or circular, sometimes
recall earlier Italian monumental graves such as those
at Caere (Cerveteri) in Etruria. The Pompeian
structures possess a certain box-like austerity, but it
is relieved by ornamentation, and diversified, especially
after the introduction of concrete techniques, by all
manner of contemporary architectural motifs. The
interiors of the tombs were magnificently painted;
and one of these edifices, closed by a single pivoted
slab of marble made to present the illusion of a double
door, contained extensive funeral furniture, including
several urns and lamps, a gold seal ring, a miniature
terracotta altar, two wine jars, and bottles of scent.

These tombs often lined the noisiest and busiest
roads. They were adjoined by benches and stalls, and
in spite of their expensive contents they were not
fenced in.

The relation between dead and living was intimate;
never more so than in AD 79 when the eruption caught
people banqueting in one of the tombs outside the
Herculaneum Gate, and they were immured for ever
inside its closed bronze portal. Petronius, whose novel
the *Satyricon* dates from the penultimate decade of
Pompeii's existence, makes his *nouveau riche* anti-hero
Trimalchio explain the sort of spirit that prompted
the erection of these memorials:

> It's a big mistake to have nice houses just for
> when you're alive and not worry about the one we
> have to live in for much longer . . . I'll put one of
> my freedmen in charge of my tomb to look after it
> and not let people run up and shit on my monument.
> I'd like you to put some ships there too, sailing
> under full canvas, and me sitting on a high platform
> in my robes of office, wearing five gold rings and
> pouring out a bagful of money for the people.[4]

The town plan of Herculaneum is much less easy to
reconstruct, because, although this always remained a
little place, there was a lot more of it than the four
blocks which are the only ones to have been completely

Opposite: Herculaneum seen from its southern corner.
In the foreground on the right, is the multi-storeyed
House of the Relief of Telephus built on the sloping spur.
Beyond, on top of the city wall, stands the sun-terrace
of the House of the Stags
Below: Fig. 4. Herculaneum

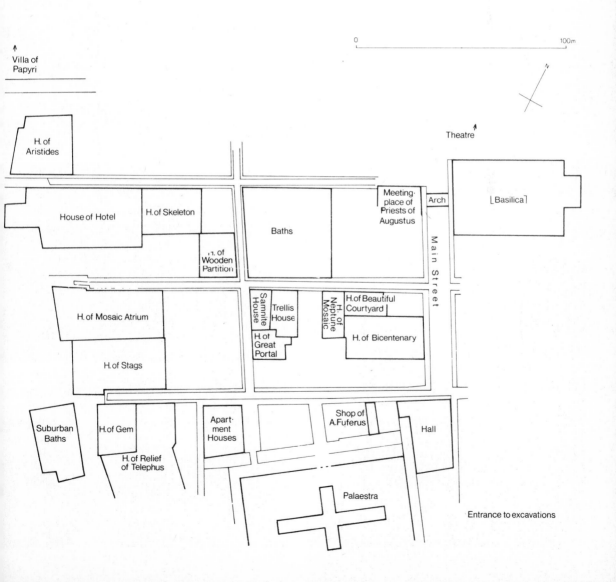

Villa of
Papyri

H. of
Aristides

House of Hotel

H. of Skeleton

H. of Mosaic Atrium

H. of Stags

Suburban
Baths

H. of Gem

H. of Relief
of Telephus

⊓. of
Wooden
Partition

Baths

Samnite
House

Trellis
House

H. of
Great
Portal

H. of
Neptune
Mosaic

H. of Beautiful
Courtyard

H. of Bicentenary

Meeting·
place of
Priests of
Augustus

Arch

Main Street

⌊Basilica⌉

Theatre

Apart·
ment
Houses

Shop of
A.Fuferus

Hall

Palaestra

Entrance to excavations

0   100m

uncovered today. They are regular, orderly and
rectangular, suggesting the influence of neighbouring
Neapolis, which was likewise built on a regular
Greek grid. The Forum of Herculaneum, which lay
to the north-east of the excavations, is still buried
deep under the modern town of Resina; and the main
artery, the *Decumanus Maximus*, has only been uncovered for a short stretch of its length. For a street in
so small a town it was remarkably wide for the period,
since its breadth, including wide pavements or
sidewalks, totalled as much as twelve metres. Vehicles
appear to have been banned on this thoroughfare, and
there can have been little traffic in other parts of
Herculaneum either, or at least little heavy traffic, for
wheel-ruts are few. At least one street was colonnaded,
like the Sacred Way at Rome after its reconstruction
by Nero.

The expansion of Herculaneum was limited by its
position on a promontory between two streams, for
the site slopes down sharply towards the south-west
in the direction of the sea.[5] At this point there were
wide terraces on massive southern ramparts resembling
medieval bastions, perforated by arches and protected
by a moat.

Opposite: The main street of Herculaneum:
the Decumanus Maximus. Perhaps the arch was the
entrance to the Forum, which is still unexcavated
Below: The town-wall at the south-western end of
Herculaneum, formerly overlooking the sea

Overleaf: The Forum at Pompeii. The triumphal arch is sometimes known as the Arch of Germanicus (with 'Arch of Caligula' beyond). On the right is the provision market (*macellum*)

Above: On the left is the Trellis House, built of cheap
rubble masonry held together by a framework of
wood, reeds or cane. At the far end rises the modern
town of Resina, under which the greater part of
Herculaneum still lies.
Opposite: The Via dell'Abbondanza, Pompeii, with
stepping-stones for pedestrians.

At Pompeii no good building stone was available; various different stones were employed in turn, and the approximate dates of successive phases of construction can be traced accordingly. In the Villa of the Mysteries outside the town six stages are detectable, and in the House of the Faun there were at least five. Until the third century BC grand buildings of this type were made of limestone from the lower Sarnus valley, cemented with clay. This material is like Roman travertine but yellower in colour, and it contains many impressions of leaves and stems. Then use was made of yellow and grey tufa, an easily worked substance which was employed for the palatial residences of the later third and second centuries BC. The less friable, fine-grained, grey type, with its handsome warmth and varied colouring, was brought from Nuceria. Mortar, including fragments of crushed tiles, was sometimes used. As in Rome, architecture gained large new opportunities when concrete appeared in the middle or later second century BC, and replaced this crushed-tile mortar. This revolutionary material opened up all the possibilities of arches and vaults, and readily took a surface of brick. Under the empire, tufa sometimes gave way to limestone again, for example in the Forum, because the latter was more receptive of the paint and stucco facings that were now required to cover columns and other surfaces.

After the earthquake of AD 62 various cheap patchwork materials came into use. The Trellis House at Herculaneum astonishingly preserves an example of flimsy, fragile *opus craticium*, based on a square lattice framework of wood and reeds or cane which is thinly covered over with a crude sort of masonry consisting of rubble, earth and plaster. Walls of the same type were also erected at Pompeii, to make partitions between shops and jutting balconies which had to be light in weight. As Vitruvius observed, this sort of construction was rapid and economical, but it involved dangers of fire and collapse.

In comparison with almost any modern town of the same size, the public buildings of Pompeii seem extraordinarily numerous and impressive.

The colonnade round the Forum at Pompeii; looking north towards Vesuvius

On the original acropolis in the so-called Triangular Forum to the south, consisting of a rock spur looking out over the sea and the mountains, scarcely anything is left of the original Doric temple. But there are extensive remains of the hundred-column portico which was built round it in the third or second century BC, after the manner of the colonnaded courts of Greek cities.

Later, the same ideas were introduced to the Forum itself. This lay below and to the west of the Triangular Forum, on one of Pompeii's few stretches of level ground. Much larger than its triangular predecessor (which should not be regarded as a true forum at all), it consisted of an oblong space, measuring 155·4 by 38 metres. Vitruvius tells us that Italian fora adopted this conformation, rather than the square shape favoured by the Greeks, in order to accommodate gladiatorial shows.[6] At first, however, the forum at Pompeii may have been irregular in shape, like those at other Samnite towns in the interior. However, in the second century BC, if not earlier, it was made completely regular and rectangular, and surrounded, like Greek market-places, by colonnades on three sides, masking shops and stalls behind. The colonnade was two-storeyed, arranged no doubt (as Vitruvius recommended) to facilitate the collection of admission fees for games and other displays held in the Forum below. The whole long and narrow enclosure was barred by gates at the ends, passing to the north under the inevitable triumphal arches.[7] Consequently, traffic could not enter; religious processions had to do without the chariots which figured in such ceremonies at Rome. It seems quite likely that Pompeii, adjoining the Greek centres on this coast, preceded Rome by a decade or two in erecting large public constructions of this kind. As far as we know, the forum of Pompeii is one of the first great architectural achievements of Italy. It is still imposing today, and when the Temple of Jupiter at its short north-western end was still standing the whole composition must have looked particularly impressive – a worthy forerunner to the Piazza San Marco in Venice.

The original colonnade, of which parts are still standing towards the southern end, was made of tufa from Nuceria. Then, to suit the taste of the empire, this was plastered over and painted (it was customary to paint columns up to a certain height). Subsequently, however, as was seen above, the desire for a smoother surface led to the decision to replace the

The Basilica of Pompeii: law court, business centre and meeting place. The most important public edifice in the town, and the earliest of such buildings that has survived anywhere

tufa by limestone. But this process had still not been completed when Pompeii came to an end.

The orderly arrangement of the colonnade was not matched by any symmetry in the buildings which faced the Forum on every side. These were a mixed collection. In addition to the trading centres, of which something will be said in Chapter 7, they included at the short south-eastern end three halls, which served municipal purposes. One of these chambers was allocated to the pair of annually elected chief officials (duoviri), who held judicial powers and administered the electoral registers and censuses. Another belonged to the second pair of principal functionaries, the aediles, who were of lesser but still considerable importance, being concerned with sanitation, roads, markets and games. And the central room, which contained shelves for books, provided the meeting-place of the town council (decuriones). In the corner outside was the Comitium, the open area in which elections for the municipal offices were held.

At the southern end of the long west side of the Forum stood the large, grand Basilica – we know this was its name because idlers have scratched up the word on an outer wall. This large hall, measuring 55 by 24 metres, was a legal, commercial, and social meeting-place, the ancestor of law courts, English stock exchanges, and Italian gallerie all in one. I have described in my Roman Forum the great Basilica Aemilia and Basilica Julia at Rome. But that city had also contained earlier basilicas, which have now vanished, and it is possible that the building at Pompeii, which seems to date from about 100 BC, owes aspects of its design to one of these.[8] Yet the Pompeian Basilica may also have been partially inspired by prototypes, likewise no longer to be seen, in Neapolis or other Greek cities of southern Italy. Basilica is a Greek word, which perhaps came from the colonnaded throne-rooms or audience-rooms of Hellenistic kings. It was these which provided the models for the halls in private Roman mansions, where, as Vitruvius describes, their noble owners conducted deliberations and private hearings and domestic trials; and the basilicas, too, may have been partially derived from the same Greek source. These buildings, which were among the ancestors of the Christian basilica church, consisted of long rectangular structures, Greek temples turned outside in – that is to say, with internal instead of external colonnades, forming two parallel rows of columns which divided a broad central nave from narrower aisles on either side.

In the Basilica at Pompeii these rows of columns, constructed of brick with a coating of stucco, were responded to by parallel two-storeyed lines of half-columns embedded in the inside face of the walls themselves. One of the short ends (on the south-eastern side) was perforated by five main entrance doors preceded by a vestibule, and the longer sides contained two lesser entrances.[9] At the short north-western end, opposite the main entrance, there was no apse, as is often to be found in basilicas elsewhere, but the right-angled extremity of the building was occupied by a two-storeyed tribunal which contained an official throne and was flanked by rooms on either side. Whether the central portion of the interior, inside the colonnades, was roofed or lay open to the heavens has been greatly disputed, but the large size of the column-stumps suggests that there was, in fact, a roof – presumably a gabled timber affair, though the ceiling beneath the gable must have been flat. If such a roof existed, the building must have been provided with its light by windows in the outer wall between the semi-columns. The walls of the interior were painted to imitate blocks of marble, in a style we shall encounter again in private houses (Chapters 5 and 6).

At Herculaneum there was also a basilica, but we can say very little about its design because it is hidden far beneath the ground; the length of this edifice is variously estimated at 38 and 61 metres, and it seems to have possessed an apse. Tunnels bored into its midst between 1739 and 1761 yielded a rich haul of objects, including a bronze horse (and the head of another) from a chariot which surmounted its exterior. But now the shafts are stuffed with rubble and closed.

Whether there was an amphitheatre at Herculaneum we do not know, though gladiators' helmets have been found in the place. But at Pompeii there was a relatively enormous arena, capable of seating almost the entire population. After its construction in 80–65 BC, the Forum was no longer needed for the staging of such fights. Sunk deep into the earth, the Pompeian amphitheatre recalls that in earlier times these open spaces had been natural hollows, with earth heaped up round their circumference. The outer wall, with a low frontage containing external steps which lead up to the top of the auditorium, is indented with arches and strengthened by great buttresses. Being already at a lower level than the surrounding terrain, the

The amphitheatre at Pompeii: the oldest known
permanent building of this kind. The external steps
lead to the upper tiers of seats

central, elliptical place of combat is not riddled with the honeycomb of substructures which in other amphitheatres served to house the wild animals needed for beast fights; though graffiti and advertisements ('Felix will fight bears') show that this form of carnage was by no means unknown at Pompeii.

depicted in stucco reliefs on his tomb; and a peculiarly distasteful form of whimsy inspired painters to represent gladiator fights between Cupids, brandishing weapons in their pudgy hands. According to another mural, a host of pedlars and stall-keepers congregated, as one might expect, in the large square outside the

Painting of a chariot-race in the amphitheatre of Pompeii. Naples Museum

Other graffiti have a lot to say about the gladiators themselves, and record their contests with one another. The Thracian Celadus is called the hero and heart-throb of the girls; and another scrawl names the net-fighter Crescens as the boss who gives the girls the medicine they need in the night. And there are sketches of gladiatorial fights, sometimes executed with a good deal of spirit and dash.

The walls of Pompeii also display a great many painted inscriptions recording contests ('3 killed, 6 spared, 9 victorious') and announcing future attractions; such posters are to be found at almost every street-corner. Some of these advertisements announce protection against the summer sun or winter rain: 'There will be awnings', referring to the canopies stretched over the seating areas and supported by masts. *Sparsiones* are also announced – meaning either free gifts or showers of scented water.

The same entertainments find their way into the subject-matter of the sculptors and artists of Pompeii. The fish-sauce merchant Marcus Umbricius Scaurus (or his heirs) had the bad taste to arrange that the gladiatorial combats he had financed should be

amphitheatre, selling food and drink and other wares from improvised tents and booths. One of the duties of the two *aediles*, the junior partners among the four officials who ruled Pompeii, was to let out concessions for refreshment stands at the games.

A further painting relating to gladiatorial affairs depicts one of the few events which brought Pompeii briefly into imperial history, because the involvement of a former Roman senator made Tacitus regard the occasion as worth describing. For in AD 59, during the reign of Nero, this Pompeian amphitheatre was the scene of a violent brawl between the local population and visitors from neighbouring Nuceria (Chapter 1). The painting from Pompeii showing the incident (to which partisan graffiti also refer) gives a bird's-eye view of the amphitheatre and displays the rioting in progress.

It arose [says the historian] out of a trifling incident at a gladiatorial show given by a man who had been expelled from the Roman senate, Livineius Regulus. During an exchange of taunts – characteristic of these disorderly country towns – abuse led to stone throwing, and then swords were drawn. The people of Pompeii, where the display was being held, came off best. Many wounded and mutilated Nucerians were taken to the capital. Many bereavements, too, were suffered by parents and children. The emperor instructed the senate to investigate the affair; and the senate passed it to the consuls. When they reported back, the senate debarred Pompeii from holding any similar gathering for ten years. Illegal associations in the town were dissolved; and Livineius and his fellow-instigators of the disorders were exiled.[10]

Painting of the amphitheatre at Pompeii. The scene shows the brawl between the people of Pompeii and Nuceria (Nocera) in AD 59 which resulted in the temporary closure of the amphitheatre. Naples Museum

However, later on the ten-year ban may have been lifted owing to the intercession of the emperor's wife Poppaea, whose mother's family were prominent citizens of Pompeii, owning the Houses of Menander and the Golden Cupid.

These horrible spectacles meant a lot to the Pompeians, who had built their amphitheatre at an unusually early date. Indeed, it actually anticipated any solidly constructed counterpart at Rome by half a century (at this time the term *amphitheatrum* had not been invented; the word *spectacula* was used to describe such buildings). It was apparently from Campania that the Romans got the idea of this type of entertainment, and a larger number of amphitheatres have been discovered in this region than in any other part of Italy. Puteoli actually had two, one of them very big: apart from the later Colosseum at Rome, it was the largest in the Roman empire – except one. And this too was in Campania, for it belonged to Capua, a particularly important centre of gladiatorial games and training – for which the healthy climate of the place was particularly well suited. The amphitheatre of Capua, in the form in which it has survived, is later than Pompeii's, but it probably replaced an earlier one which had been senior to the Pompeian arena in date.

Gladiators were evidently one of the legacies Campania obtained from the Samnites. Down to the first century BC, 'gladiator' and 'Samnite' were synonymous terms; and then the latter became the name of a particular type of gladiator. Tomb paintings in Samnium dating from soon after 400 BC had already depicted gladiatorial combats, including a scene (found in 1954) showing a gladiator who is mortally wounded. The ancient historian Nicolaus of Damascus believed that Rome derived the institution from the Etruscans,[11] and they are, indeed, likely to have been the ultimate source. But the Samnites were very probably intermediaries, passing the custom on to Rome by way of Campania.

Objections to this form of amusement in the ancient world are depressingly scarce. But they did exist, and the most noteworthy protest comes from the pen of Seneca, the philosopher who was also Nero's minister. His words did not pass unnoticed by the gladiators at Pompeii, for a graffito on the dining-room wall of their barracks records that 'the philosopher Annaeus Senecas' (an inaccurate version of his name, indicating the hand of a foreigner) 'is the only Roman writer to condemn the bloody Games'.[12]

Gladiator's helmet from Pompeii. Naples Museum

These barracks have yielded extensive finds. In addition to the remains of numerous people who were killed in the eruption (Chapter 2), very many weapons have been discovered in the rooms opening onto the portico. These finds include fifteen helmets and six shoulder-protectors.

The barracks were housed in a building which did not adjoin the amphitheatre, as might have been expected, but stood next to the Large Theatre. Originally these quarters, and the large square colonnade round which they centred, had actually formed an annex of the theatre, in accordance with the indication of Vitruvius that theatres should possess an adjunct of this kind, where audiences might shelter from the rain and preparations could be made for performances.

This Large Theatre of Pompeii, like its amphitheatre, is older than any counterpart at Rome – indeed apparently much earlier, since the first stone theatre in the capital, constructed by Pompey, dates from 55 BC, whereas the building at Pompeii appears to go back, in its first durable form, to the second if not the third century BC. Perhaps the town had possessed an earlier theatre, with wooden seating, even before

The Gladiators' barracks in the colonnaded court of the Large Theatre at Pompeii

hat time, but at any rate it seems to have been round about 200 BC that seats of tufa were introduced. They were built into a natural hollow, which was made into a half circle round the *orchestra* where the actors performed. These seating arrangements, following the original slope of the hillside, were Greek in character; and recent excavations have made it possible to compare this Pompeii theatre with a more or less contemporary example of another Greek plan, likewise in an Italian setting, at a place in the interior of Samnium. There at Pietrabbondante – the ancient name has not yet been identified[13] – the theatre, constructed of well-joined, polygonal, limestone masonry, was not modified by subsequent alterations, so that we can see what it looked like from the beginning. At Pompeii, on the other hand, in the time of Sulla (who died in 78 BC), a large ornate back-wall, after the Roman fashion, was added in front of the *orchestra*. Later on further alterations were made, and when the theatre assumed its final form in imperial times, all the acting took place up on the stage in front of the wall, so that the *orchestra* was no longer used by the performers but became available for supplementary seating instead.

The drama was not, of course, as greatly favoured by the people of Pompeii as the amphitheatre. But a mass of graffiti shows that it was immensely popular all the same. The admiration lavished on one actor, Paris (who has been identified with Nero's friend and favourite Lucius Domitius Paris), is revealed by a whole series of graffiti: 'Comrades of the Paris Club'; 'Paris pearl of the stage' (on a tomb); 'Paris the sweet darling'; 'Good for Paris'; 'Purpurio, with the Paris fans'. Another member of the same profession, Norbanus Sorex of the late first century BC, is the subject of one of the most brilliant bronze portrait busts of the age, found in the Temple of Isis. It is an animated head, and must have looked even more striking before the brilliantly coloured eyeballs and jewel-like white of the eyes were taken away. Sorex is not perhaps very likeable; but he is highly individual, the sort of man who would brush criticism aside. There is also record of a successful visit to Pompeii by a performer called Actius; and we hear of an actress named Rotica or Erotica. As for the ravaged, dramatic, bust which used wrongly to be labelled 'Seneca', a bronze masterpiece found in the Villa of the Papyri outside Herculaneum, it probably represents a tragic actor – or possibly a playwright, though if so he was surely not a local product but one of the earlier Greeks from other lands whose plays were so eagerly followed at these towns. Their eagerness is shown very clearly by the frequency with which upper-class householders directed that the walls of their rooms should be painted with theatrical scenes. This taste became greatly accentuated under the theatre-loving Nero. But even without that imperial impulse, Augustus Hare, most beguiling of nineteenth-century travel writers, was justified in concluding that 'the rage for plays, which still distinguishes the Neapolitans, existed in Pompeii'.

Above: Head of a leading actor at Pompeii: Norbanus Sorex. The eyes are missing. Found in the Temple of Isis, and now in the Naples Museum

Opposite: Formerly identified as Seneca, but probably a tragic actor; a famous portrait known from a number of copies in bronze (of which this example is made) and in marble. From the Villa of the Papyri outside Herculaneum. Naples Museum

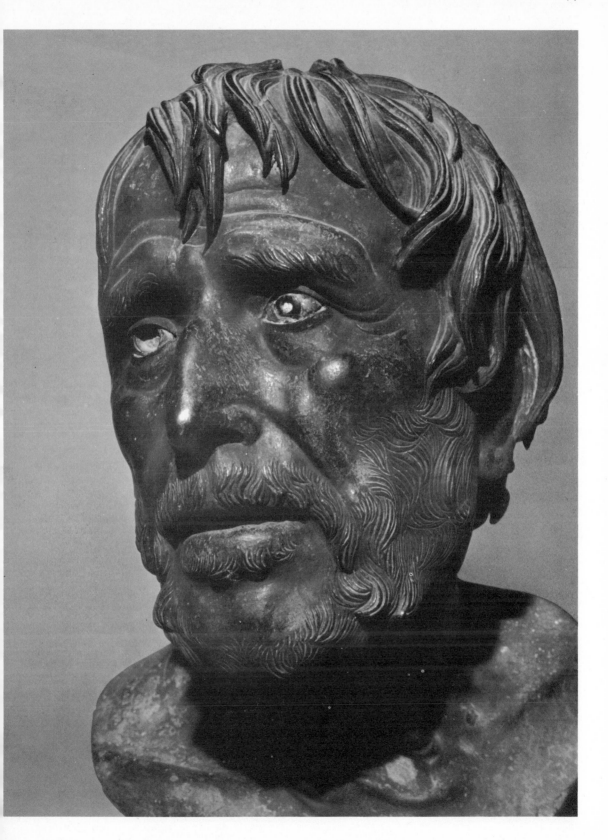

Opposite – upper picture: The small Theatre, or Odeon, at Pompeii, originally roofed
Opposite – lower picture: The rounded end of the Odeon auditorium. The gate leads through to the Large Theatre
Below: Model of the Theatre, Herculaneum: reached by tunnels in the eighteenth century and still underground today

Moreover, next door to the Large Theatre, the elite of the place were able to enjoy the amenities of a much smaller counterpart, the so-called Odeon. Dating from 80 to 75 BC – the first period of the Roman colony – this little auditorium, still excellently preserved, had room only for between 1,000 and 1,500 spectators, since it was intended for intimate concerts, performances and recitations. The Odeon was covered over, though the way in which this was done is disputed; and so is the question whether what we see today represents a once-and-for-all plan or an original design modified by subsequent insertions. At the extremities of the rows of seats, forming the heads of their side parapets, the supports consist of finely sculptured male figures, a feature also found at the Samnite town Pietrabbondante.[14]

The Theatre at Herculaneum is a subject almost too painful to write about. Between the years 1702 and 1715 it was discovered by Emmanuel Maurice of Lorraine, Prince d'Elboeuf – an Austrian general in the Neapolitan service. He sent tunnelling parties deep and far beneath the ground. What the tunnellers discovered was a superbly preserved theatre of great magnificence, not backed against the slope, but built on its own as at Neapolis and Rome, with its stage resting upon a double order of arches and pillars. This theatre was lavishly adorned with columns, statuary, and polychrome marbles. It is astonishing that a little town of 5,000 people should boast a theatre, or indeed any urban organization, on such a scale. For seven years d'Elboeuf plundered the precious remains of this building, sending them away in all directions; the best of the statues went to Prince Charles Eugene of Savoy.[15] The looting continued with little or no attention to the archaeological considerations that would apply today. Well may J. J. Deiss, in his book on Herculaneum, conclude that the plundering of this monument was 'perhaps the greatest tragedy of the theatre'.

More skilful and sensitive hands were at work between 1738 and 1777, but it has never proved possible to clear the building, which still remains entombed beneath the gigantic onslaught of the eruption. It can, however, by special permission, be reached – by a staircase descending twenty-seven metres into the dank depths: the descent which inspired horror in Charles Dickens (Chapter 2).

The open-air sports ground or 'Palaestra' at Herculaneum is as imposingly and disproportionately large as the theatre. It included an ample, apsed meeting hall and a cross-shaped central swimming

Apsed hall, originally vaulted, opening off the centre of the columned portico of the sports ground (Palaestra) at Herculaneum. The olive crowns, and other prizes of the victors, were laid on the table

pool. The pool is now a strange sight, since the vast masses of earth under which it was buried have been hollowed out to reveal its centre-piece, which is a splendid, multiple-headed giant serpent, coiled round a two-metre-high bronze tree. There is also a second, smaller palaestra at Herculaneum, forming part of the Forum Baths.

There are likewise two of these sports grounds at Pompeii. The larger one near the amphitheatre, which again contains a central swimming pool, is almost square (140 × 130 metres). All round the open space stood colonnades, and there was a double line of trees; their roots have left holes, and plaster casts poured into the hollows show that they were planes.

The small, earlier palaestras in both towns were probably inspired by the amenities of Greek gymnasia in neighbouring Neapolis. Vitruvius remarks that throughout Republican times such constructions remained rare in Italy. But then vast athletics centres were erected in many places. This major effort was a product of Augustus' Youth Movement, the *Juventus*, initiated at Rome and copied in other Italian towns. The young men were organized into local units which paraded ceremonially in public, specializing in a complicated equestrian manoeuvre; they also took part in competitive games and sports before their elders. Graffiti at the Large Palaestra at Pompeii prove that this was the local seat of the Augustan organization, which was known as the *Schola Juventutis*, or *Collegium Juvenum*. Herculaneum, too, as we can read in one of those puzzling translations that afflict even the best Italian books, 'civilly and sportingly looked after the organisations of its Juventus'. In modern times rational discussion of this institution has been difficult, since Mussolini deliberately revived and adapted it to his own purposes; and Augustus was consequently regarded as a sort of proto-Fascist. Perhaps there is a certain measure of justification for this view, granted the totally different backgrounds; at any rate he welded the young men of Italy to his regime by this organized blend of amusement and training. However, the Campanians cannot have regarded this phenomenon as altogether new, because their ancestors, in the Samnite epoch, had already possessed their own rather similar upper-class semi-military athletic clubs, called *Vereiia* or *Verehia*, 'Gate-wardens' (from an Oscan word meaning gate). It was largely for this *jeunesse dorée* that the first palaestras at Pompeii and Herculaneum, the smaller ones, had been created.

Their larger successors were the forerunners of the magnificent sports centres which later adorned the massive baths of Rome. And these Imperial Baths also owed a great deal to the public baths which had already been installed in smaller towns such as Pompeii and Herculaneum. Such establishments, like the amphitheatre and theatre of Pompeii, existed a long time before anything of the sort could be found at the capital. For example, the cold room of the Stabian Baths at Pompeii has a dome six metres in diameter, with a large circular opening, which dates from the time of Sulla (early first century BC), and has a claim to be regarded as the earliest known dome in a building of Roman Italy.[16] The baths in the Vesuvian cities do not boast the mature, rational designs of their vast successors at Rome, but they are skilfully planned all the same.

Fig. 5. The Forum Baths, Pompeii

Altogether four sets of buildings of this kind have been identified at Pompeii, the Stabian, Forum, Central and Amphitheatre Baths – the last named were reburied soon after their discovery. At Herculaneum there are two such establishments, the Forum and Suburban Baths. They give us better and more complete information about this type of institution than we possess from anywhere else in the Roman world. The basic structure of such baths (sometimes repeated and duplicated in a women's section) comprises a dressing room and then a series of chambers getting progressively hotter, first the cold room *(frigidarium)*, next a transit room to provide gradual acclimatization to the heat *(tepidarium)*, and then a hot room *(calidarium)* furnished with a basin, tubs and often a swimming pool. Sometimes there is also a sweating-room *(laconicum)*. This last refinement, intended for people with bad livers, is found only in the Central Baths of Pompeii and the Suburban Baths of Herculaneum – both of which institutions were built during the last days of their town. The little *laconica*, lit by paned oval windows and a skylight, recall Seneca's almost contemporary criticism of all the new kinds of luxuries which were creeping into the public baths, among which he particularly

Opposite: Hot room in the Forum Baths, Pompeii. Floors and walls are hollow for the passage of hot air. The basin bears a date: AD 3–4.
Below: Vaulted dressing room for women in the Forum Baths, Herculaneum, with racks for clothing

mentions windows. Pompeii and Herculaneum, it is true, do not (as far as we know at present) match the various amenities and fine views and sunbathing facilities to which his description refers, but all the same these latest bathing places do introduce a number of significant novelties in addition to the *laconicum*. For example, the Central Baths at Pompeii, which were never completed, show a new consistency of lay-out. And in the recently excavated Suburban Baths of Herculaneum, the best preserved of all these thermal complexes, one of a number of notable features is a small colonnaded atrium displaying two superimposed rows of arches which rise straight up from their capitals without horizontal architraves.

Above: The atrium of the Suburban Baths at Herculaneum. The arches rise straight from the columns.
Opposite: Inside the Nolan Gate, Pompeii

Although not altogether unparalleled at the time, this is a feature which never became characteristic of classical architecture, [17] and which came into its own only at the outset of the Middle Ages; later it was typical of Romanesque cathedrals.

Since baths had to be resistant to great heat, they needed fire-proof ceilings, and it was consequently in this type of building, for which wooden roofs would be useless and dangerous, that the Romans developed and exploited the science of concrete-based vaulting. Thus the little vaults in the Vesuvian cities are forerunners of the gigantic arches and cupolas and apses of the enormous imperial baths and palaces of the capital. The vaulting is adorned with elegant stucco work – less perishable than painting, though the damp atmosphere must quite rapidly have affected the stucco as well – and the pools, together with the niches and vaults above them, are covered with blue mosaics diversified by marine animals. Elbow-rests show sculpted chimeras and dolphins, and lavatory seats shone with precious marble.

The central heating to be seen in the baths of Pompeii and Herculaneum was invented early in the first century BC by Gaius Sergius Orata[18] (who owed his surname to a fondness for a seafish, the *aurata*). In earlier times there had been only large bronze braziers. These were still retained thereafter in the men's *tepidarium* at the Forum Baths of Pompeii (though not in the corresponding room for women). But generally, from now on, the pavements of *calidaria* and *tepidaria* were raised on small brick columns, and the cavities thus formed were filled with hot air distributed from furnaces so as to raise the temperature by $30°$. This figure could be doubled by extending the hot air upwards into similar cavities in the walls.

It was transmitted through pipes or hollow bricks; and, in the hot rooms at least, further pipes were inserted into the ceilings as well. In the Pompeian Forum Baths the furnace, fed by charcoal, was placed in the middle between the men's and women's wings. Much can also be learnt about the technical arrangements from private baths in the Villa Rustica and other country houses at Boscoreale.

At most of the principal public baths there was a women's section as well as a men's. But at the Suburban Baths of Herculaneum there was not. When no such segregation was provided for, the sexes were probably allotted separate times. This was not, however, always the case in the great cities, where mixed bathing sometimes prevailed until Hadrian, in the

Stucco decoration in the Stabian Baths at Pompeii. This graceful art form, which also played a large part in private houses, is seen at its best in the Baths of these towns

second century AD, forbade the practice. Women were easily subject to criticism in the baths. Petronius and Juvenal have a lot to say about the improprieties that might occur, and these are also dwelt upon by pornographic graffiti in Pompeii and Herculaneum (though one graffitist, in the Forum Baths at the latter place, clothes such sentiments more poetically in a eulogy addressed to Ovid, author of the *Art of Love*).

The baths normally opened at midday, the time when the furnaces were lit; at Rome, Hadrian put the hour forward to 2 p.m. except for invalids. The opening was announced by bells or gongs or by an announcement shouted by slaves; at Pompeii, where the baths were mostly located at street intersections, the moment must have become rapidly known to all. In some towns, especially where the facilities fell short of the demand, these establishments were not only accessible for the rest of the day, but also remained open for some hours during the night; and this was evidently the case at Pompeii, where over 1,300 lamps have been found in the Forum Baths.

Bathers did not carry soap, which was not in common use, being reserved for medical treatment of sores and for use as a hair-dye; the elder Pliny describes it as 'an invention of the Gauls for giving a reddish tint to the hair'.[19] But those who frequented the baths were expected to bring their own oil and soda, and scrapers, and various sorts of towels. They were also accompanied by numbers of slaves, who must have found it hard to fit into these small rooms, so different from the massive halls in the later imperial baths of the capital. Indeed, even at Rome, as Juvenal pointed out, people who took too large a retinue when they went bathing were a nuisance; for example:

That show-off Tongilius, who's such a bore at the baths
With his mob of ruddy retainers and his outsize oil-flask
Of rhinoceros-horn.[20]

But bathing, of course, was by no means all that could be done at the baths. They were also clubs and sporting associations and a great deal besides. They were intensely active and noisy. Seneca had good reason to know this, because he once had lodgings right over a public bath-house; and he gives a harrowing description of the continual row made by people splashing, massaging and being massaged, playing ball games, brawling, advertising their services as hair removers, selling drinks and sausages and pastries, or merely enjoying the noise of their own singing as they took their baths.[21]

The men's hot room at the Forum Baths, Herculaneum. In addition to the heating below the floor, terracotta hot-pipes were laid in the walls; one can be seen on the left, and in the right wall, beside the apse, is a vertical indentation for a pipe

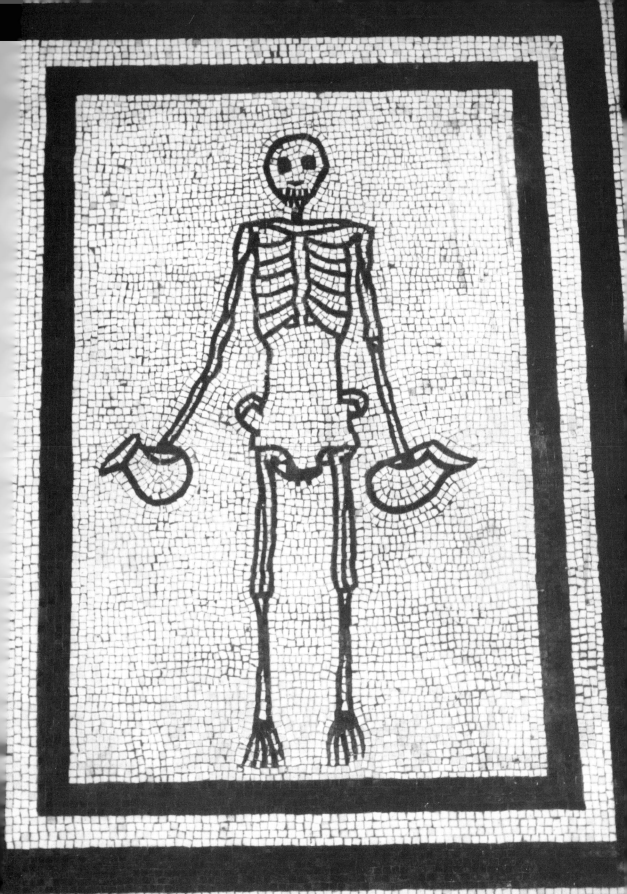

4. Temples; Gods and Goddesses; and Philosophers

As in all ancient towns, life at Pompeii and Herculaneum was inextricably bound up with religion of various kinds, official, emotional, and private. No temples have yet been discovered at Herculaneum,[1] but that is only because such a relatively small part of the town has been excavated. At Pompeii ten temples have come to light.

Of the sixth century BC Doric temple on the southern spur, known as the Triangular Forum, hardly anything is left, either from the original edifice or from its various Samnite and Roman reconstructions.[2]

Opposite: Mosaic of a skeleton from Pompeii. A further mosaic shows a skull. Both are intended as exhortations to enjoy life while you can. Naples Museum
Below: Hercules was revered but also mocked; statue of the god, drunk, in the House of the Stags, Herculaneum

The original temple had probably been dedicated to Heracles (Hercules), who was very popular with merchants because of his long journeys and may have been regarded as the founder of Pompeii, just as he was also believed to have founded Herculaneum. The Samnites, too, were especially devoted to his cult. Then, in the final years of the town, wall-paintings display a new and fashionable interest in the mythological theme of the infant Hercules strangling snakes. One of the reasons why this story received attention was because emperors, notably Nero, liked to be regarded as reincarnations of Hercules – the man who had risen by merit to be a god. Yet it had always been permissible, also, to regard Hercules as a fine figure of fun; Euripides had portrayed him humorously in the *Alcestis* five centuries earlier, and Herculaneum mocks its divine founder by a sculpture which shows him drunkenly attempting to urinate. Silenus, too, is displayed in an apparently drunken state on a relief adorning a fountain.

Another important and ancient Pompeian shrine, slightly better preserved though still in very poor condition, is the Temple of Apollo, which stands within a precinct flanking half of the long south-western side of the Forum. The axis of the building slightly deviates from the line of the present Forum; that is to say the temple preceded the Forum in date. Its first traces go back to the sixth century BC, the period when the cult was introduced, no doubt from Cumae which possessed a famous oracle of Apollo. His worship was also transmitted to Dicaearchia (Puteoli) and Neapolis, and the latter city may have been the intermediary responsible for the coming of Apollo to Pompeii. His temple, it appears, then became the principal sanctuary of the town, replacing the shrine of Heracles. The oldest remains and surviving layout of the building date from the fifth century, when either the Greeks or Samnites were engaged in its restoration and reconstruction. The portico of the

Overleaf: The Temple of Apollo, Pompeii. The statue of Apollo the Archer is a copy of a bronze sculpture found on the site, and now in the Naples Museum

cloister, a colonnade of forty-eight columns, was added some three hundred years later. It recalls a contemporary precinct at Gabii near Rome, except that this colonnade, unlike the Gabian one, runs right round the back in Greek style; though the high pedestal of the Pompeian temple recalls Italian rather than Greek models. Under Augustus, no doubt, the cult received a marked impetus, because he declared Apollo to be his patron.[3]

The classical Greek god, in all his splendour as the lord of civilization, is displayed by a bronze statue of Apollo the Archer, which was found on the site of the temple. Another statue, depicting him as Lyre-Player, was found in the House of the Citharist (Lyre-Player). Both these effigies are now in the Naples Museum, though a copy of the Archer has been placed in the precinct of the temple where it was found.

When the Romans built their first shrine of Apollo in the capital, in *c.* 433–431 BC, they already knew him as an oracular god, associated with the Sibylline oracles brought to Rome from Cumae in the previous century, but owing to the pestilence currently afflicting the city they now chose to narrow his role to that of the divine Healer. Four hundred years later, however, Augustus transformed him into the brilliant Greek god of peace and enlightenment, adapted to the patriotic and propagandist purposes of Rome and himself, and from that time onwards, in the Apolline Games which started at Pompeii on every 5 July, the link with the regime was duly stressed. Apollo was intended, as R.M. Ogilvie remarks, 'to epitomise everything that was new and young – and successful'. Nero, too, as an enthusiastic lyre-player and man of culture, was strongly devoted to Apollo, and after the earthquake which devastated Pompeii in AD 62 during his reign (Chapter 2) steps were taken to repair the damage to this temple. Certain changes were now made; the previous Ionic columns were altered to Corinthian, and the two-storeyed colonnade was replaced by a single-storey portico faced with stucco.

Nevertheless, by this time Pompeii had passed from the patronage of Apollo into the special protection of Venus. Of her great temple, dominating the plain from an elevated terrace at the south-western corner of the town, nothing survives, because it was so severely injured in the earthquake of AD 62 that the decision was taken to demolish and reconstruct the building completely – no doubt on a magnificent scale, because, through his adoptive ancestor Caesar, the reigning emperor Nero claimed to be descended from Venus. But when the eruption came seventeen years later, this major project had not got beyond the preparatory stage of erecting huge masonry bases reinforced with clamp-irons.

However, the influence of the goddess had exercised a very pervasive effect upon Pompeian life. In the first place, the people concerned with thoughts of love continually brought her name into the graffiti they

Above: Bronze statue of Apollo from the House of the Citharist, Pompeii. From a mid-fifth-century BC original
Opposite: One of the countless pictures of Venus Pompeiana, patron goddess of the town; a sign outside the shop of the cloth merchant Verecundus

scrawled on the walls. Sometimes the spirit is critical; one discontented man, writing on the wall of the Basilica, wants to smash her guts.[4] (A painter in the House of Menander shows her as an ugly, hairy old woman.) Another graffitist asks: 'What is the use of having a Venus if she's made of marble?' For these scrawlers on walls testify to a widespread feeling that Venus must guarantee their success in love, or else she deserves to be blamed (Chapter 8).

But she was more to the Pompeians than the goddess of love. She was also the mistress of nature, the mother of the universe. Interpretations of this kind did not play a large part in her Roman cult (which allotted her annual festival to dealers in vegetables and herbs) but this was her primary role in her shrine at Eryx in Sicily, the great shrine of Aphrodite with whom the Roman deity came to be identified. This, too, was the mighty conception of Lucretius:

Darling of Gods and Men, beneath the gliding stars
You fill rich earth and buoyant sea with your
    presence,
For every living thing achieves its life through
    you. . . .
Everywhere, through all seas, mountains and
    waterfalls,
Love caresses all hearts and kindles all creatures
In overmastering lust and ordained renewals.[5]

When Pompeian inscriptions describe Venus as
'*fisica*',[6] it is tempting to suppose that this word, even
if (as is possible) its real origins had been Italian and
Umbrian, was regarded as coming from the Greek
word *physis* meaning nature; and that Venus Physica
is therefore a reflection of the Lucretian sort of
concept – especially as the poet has been supposed to
have had connections with this area.

At the time when he wrote his poem, the name of
Venus had been incorporated in the title of Sulla's
colony, which was known as 'Colonia Veneria'. In
Pompeii the goddess is everywhere, and is envisaged

at every stage of feeling between the grandiose
identification with nature and the simpler idea that if
one is crossed in love it is she who deserves to be
beaten. In 1952 the House of the Venus Marina
disclosed a colourful painting of the goddess floating
on a sea-shell escorted by two of her ever-popular
Cupids. The theme of the picture foreshadows a much
greater masterpiece by Botticelli, though at Pompeii
the divinity does not stand upright, as she does in the
Florentine picture, but floats at full length.

Her image is endlessly repeated not only in houses
but on the painted signs of taverns and shops. A
placard at a wool shop shows her on a pillar with
Cupid by her side, accompanied by a processional
scene in which her image is carried by four bearers to
an altar. A cloth-maker, Vecilius Verecundus, por-
trays her in a chariot drawn by four elephants. 'Vote
for me,' reads an election poster, 'and the Venus of
Pompeii will bring success to everything you under-
take.' The Venus of ancient Pompeii was the forerunner of the town's most sacred object in our own
time, which is an old, much restored painting of the

Sleeping figure of Venus's son Cupid; the curls were
originally painted red.
House of the Beautiful Courtyard, Herculaneum

Venus doing up her sandal; inlaid polychrome marble
(*opus sectile*) from Pompeii. Naples Museum

Madonna on the high altar of the Sanctuary of the Madonna del Rosario. And statuettes of Our Lady of Pompeii are still very lucky images in the Neapolitan area.

However, the highest patron of Pompeii was neither Hercules nor Apollo nor Venus, but the supreme Roman god Jupiter, presiding over his temple at the short north-western end of the Forum, where part of its shell is still to be seen. Probably the original divinity of the market square had been the Italian high god Mars, and we can imagine, though conjecturally, that there was an early temple of that deity on the site in about the third century BC, perhaps with its upper parts made of wood. In any case, however, as in other Italian towns, a temple of Jupiter was established in its place before 100 BC.

Its present remains, however, belong to a slightly later period. An Italian note is firmly struck by the lofty, three-metre-high base and the deep porch, on which the columns were no doubt, as elsewhere in the country, surmounted by a gabled pediment much steeper than would be found in Greece. It was at this time that the temple became the Capitolium, modelled on the great shrine of Rome founded by an Etruscan dynasty in the remotely antique period of the sixth century BC. As at Rome, the Pompeian temple was dedicated to the worship of Juno and Minerva in addition to Jupiter, though here, in this much smaller building, they share a single chapel *(cella)* – a wide chamber with an internal colonnade – instead of possessing three distinct and adjoining chapels like the Roman Capitoline temple. Why these three Capitoline deities were grouped together in a 'triad' is an unsolved question;[7] but at any rate they became the joint protectors of the Roman state, and Rome celebrated games in their honour on 1 September every year. The institution was copied by the towns of Italy – including Pompeii.

The inner walls of its temple of Jupiter were painted in imitation of marble veneer, and the massive base contained rooms which housed sacrificial offerings, and the town's public treasury. In the earthquake of AD 62, as we can see from the relief in the House of Lucius Caecilius Jucundus, the columns crashed

Water-colour painting showing restoration of the Temple of Jupiter beside the Forum of Pompeii

down, dragging with them the splendid pediment and all its glittering adornments. And one of the columns killed a workman. At the time of the eruption in 79 the building had not yet come into use again, and remained in a ruined condition; a statue was still lodged in the crypt.

During the interval the cult seems to have been transferred to a much smaller shrine 265 metres to the south-east, where images of Jupiter and Juno and a bust of Minerva have been found. This temporary residence of the Capitoline worship was the temple of Jupiter Milichius, Zeus seen as the 'easily entreated', from whom pious people hoped for benefits. The Greeks of Sicily favoured this cult, and it was particularly related to agriculture, which was the principal activity of Pompeii.[8]

Round the Forum, near the principal temple of the Capitoline divinities, other shrines can be seen. None of their remains are at all extensive, but it has been possible to identify the municipal or patriotic aims to which they were devoted.

One such building was dedicated to the *Lares Publici*, the protectors of the town. 'At once homely and formidable, beautiful and touchy', in the words of Marcel Brion, they were identified with the deified spirits of dead ancestors. Their cult was paralleled by *lararia* in every private house and major cross-roads, and at Rome this latter manifestation was cunningly reorganized by Augustus in such a way as to link the worship with his own person.

Another reference to the first emperor appeared in the title of a further temple, very close to the shrine of the *Lares;* for it is dedicated to Fortuna Augusta (3 BC). Fortuna, the bringer of fertility and increase, was an ancient agricultural deity who in 194 BC had been brought from Antium (Anzio) or Praeneste (Palestrina) to Rome, where she was given a temple. First she became identified with the Greek Fortune (Tyche), the patron-goddess of cities who was widely revered as the presiding deity of good luck. Then, when the empire started, the addition of the epithet 'Augusta' to her name indicated her indelible association with the regime.

Lower down on the same side of the Forum stood a temple devoted to the imperial cult itself. It may originally have been dedicated to Augustus, but the surviving ruins date from a later building devoted to the Genius of Vespasian, whose death preceded the obliteration of Pompeii itself by only one month. His

Above: Coin of Vespasian (AD 69–79), whose temple stands beside the Forum at Pompeii
Opposite: Altar of the Temple of Vespasian (who died a month before the eruption) depicting a sacrificial scene

statue could be seen in the niche at the back of the building; and there still survives an altar which is a worthy specimen of the official art of the day. One side of its surface is decorated with reliefs of a sacrificial scene, showing a priest and his assistant, an attendant *(lictor)*, a flute-player and other young men; and on the other side are representations of the oak-wreath and laurel-branches decreed by the Roman senate to Augustus. The imperial cult had its own special priests, part-time like those of other Roman cults: they were the Augustales, who also tended a shrine in the Pompeian Provision Market or *Macellum* and were equally active at Herculaneum, where they possessed a *collegium* or Association on the main street.

Far more excitement was generated by the Egyptian goddess Isis, whose place of worship stood some distance away to the south-east of the Forum, near the Temple of Jupiter Milichius and the theatres. The best preserved of the shrines of Pompeii, it would have looked more impressive than it does if the early excavators had not taken away so many of their finds – decorations, furniture and paintings – and deposited them at the museum at Portici, now transferred to Naples. These objects represent our main source of

information for the cult; they also inspired Bulwer Lytton to long descriptions in *The Last Days of Pompeii*, and instigated Madame Blavatsky, founder of the Theosophic Society, to write her book *Isis Unveiled*.

Surrounded by a high wall, with a single entrance located in such a way that the ceremonies could not be seen from outside, the precinct contained a number of separate structures. In addition to the temple itself they included a little shrine displaying stucco reliefs and giving access to a subterranean reservoir of holy Nile water. There was also a covered repository for the debris of sacrifices; an initiation hall; a room for meetings and banquets; and a few lodgings for priests. In the earthquake of AD 62 the temple was almost wholly destroyed. But its subsequent reconstruction was defrayed by Numerius Popidius Celsinus, member of a leading Pompeian family, who, although only six years of age, was consequently elected a member of the town council 'without charge'. When the eruption came, the priests, interrupted at lunch, did their best to save all the valuables. But they died in the attempt, as was described in Chapter 2.

The worship of Isis was one of the 'mystery' religions which seemed to innumerable men and women of the time to be all that made life worth living. In a reaction against a certain tedium and emptiness in their quiet, well-ordered, materialistic existence, people attached themselves to divine saviours, independent of official, patriotic religion. Such a saviour, in addition to giving them, as individuals, strength and holiness to endure their life upon earth, was expected, when that life was done, to endow his or her faithful servants with a happy after-life, beyond and above the frightening decrees of oppressive Fate or Fortune. It is true that magical practices, of which there were very many at Pompeii,[9] might also help to trick Fate. But saviour-cults were far more satisfactory to the emotions. Unlike the official Roman worships, they had their own full-time priests who organized thrilling, sensational ceremonials, binding their congregations to the divinity and assuaging their anxieties by a solemn, long-drawn-out series of progressive initiations, accompanied by purifying rituals and sacramental feasts.

The most popular of all the mystery worships was that of Isis – the only pagan religion that ever stood some chance of becoming universal. And it is not surprising that this cult was particularly popular in Pompeii, where numerous paintings and inscriptions show signs of Egyptian influence, either religious or commercial or aesthetic. This influence was encouraged by proximity to the main trade route from Alexandria to Puteoli. At Rome, for a long time, there were official doubts about the respectability of Isis owing to moral and political suspicions of Ptolemaic Egypt; but after the annexation of the country by Augustus in 30 BC these fears were gradually allayed, and from the time of Caligula (AD 38) the capital, too, had its permanent temple of Isis. In 69 her priests gained favour with the new Flavian dynasty by saving the life of the young Domitian, who became a devotee of the goddess.

Her cult incorporated the mythical ancient lore of Egypt, and her companion Osiris represented not only the origin of civilization but the birth and death of the year. The Festival of the Finding of Osiris, which lasted from 12 November to 14 November, and the Procession of the Boat on 5 March, were the occasions for exuberant, emotional rejoicing, stage-managed with dramatic force. Unlike other shrines, the Temple of Isis was open every day, and there were always impressive services. The first was at dawn, to celebrate the resurrection of Osiris, god of the underworld, and the daily rebirth of the Sun; and every afternoon there was a benediction and offering of water, the fecund source and perpetuation of all life. The glamour of the enchantress deity, hailed as the Glory of Women and the Goddess of Ten Thousand Names, is revealed in an intense personal experience of the novelist, orator and magician Apuleius from North Africa, who woke in sudden terror to see her dazzling apparition rising before him beneath the full moon.[10] And some of the same excitement is conveyed by a painting from Herculaneum, which dramatically depicts the elaborate daily Rites of the Water, accompanied by music and chanting and the burning of incense.

Another mystery cult, which could not claim the legendary antiquity of Egyptian lore but had already played a major part in early Greece, was centred round Dionysus (Bacchus). He was the god of wine, but he was also the disturbing liberator of mankind, symbolizing the irrational, irrepressible elements in human nature. From the possessed initiate he demanded ferocious single-mindedness, but in return he offered escape from worldly reality into mystic communion, and the promise of the blessed life after death for which the adherents of all these religions so greatly longed. After sweeping through Greece in the sixth

A painting from Herculaneum showing white-robed priests of Isis
performing their afternoon service, the Ceremony of the Water. Naples Museum

Above: Pediment from the Samnite Temple of the
Dionysian deities outside Pompeii, *c.* 200 BC.
Dionysus (Bacchus) and Ariadne are flanked by Silenus and
Cupid. Pompeii Museum

Opposite: Bacchic scene in the House of the Dioscuri,
Pompeii
Below: Wall-painting in the Villa of the Mysteries
outside Pompeii: the central scene (much damaged) of
Dionysus reclining on Ariadne's lap

century BC, the worship of Dionysus or Bacchus was
destined, two and three hundred years later, to
become the distinctive worship of the Hellenistic age,
the epoch of the huge kingdoms of Alexander the
Great's heirs. And, in particular, the cult had an
enormous vogue in southern Italy, where these
mysteries, identifying the god with the old Italian
deity Liber, were widely popular in the early second
century BC, after Rome had defeated Hannibal and
was starting to look towards the east.

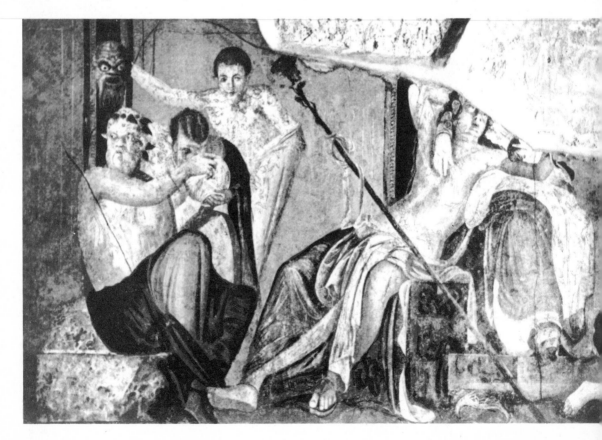

In 1947 the remains of a shrine of Bacchus of this period came to light just to the south of Pompeii, on the hill of Sant' Abbondio.[11] The pediment, which is preserved in Pompeii's museum, displays seated figures of Bacchus and Ariadne. The god found Ariadne abandoned on the island of Naxos, and made her his bride, endowing her with eternal life just as his devotees, too, would win immortality for themselves. And she also symbolized the vital attraction that this cult, like the worship of Isis but unlike the Olympian or Roman religions, exercised upon women.

Very soon after this temple had been built, the Roman senate clamped down on the rites of Bacchus or Dionysus, regarding such emotional excesses as a threat to public order. But thereafter the faith flooded into the Roman world, and by the following century, though still unofficial, the worship of Dionysus was transformed into a respectable and widespread mystery religion. In Pompeii it evidently had a great many devotees – and gave some of them a serious spiritual experience.

One such man, evidently, was the painter of a room in the large Villa of the Mysteries (Villa Item), outside the Herculaneum Gate of Pompeii. The room, which measures five by seven metres and opens onto an open terrace, appears to have formed part of the private apartments of the master and mistress of the house. But three walls of this room are covered with the greatest single group of paintings that has come down to us from anywhere in the ancient world. Dating from the time of Augustus or a little earlier (Chapter 6), they relate to the cult of Bacchus.

It is easy to give a wrong idea of their intention, because unfortunately the wall displaying the most important pictures is also the only one which is substantially damaged, in its most vital, central part. As the visitor entered by a wide doorway in one of the shorter sides, this is the wall that confronted him. Straight ahead in the very middle of the picture he saw Ariadne, seated high and erect, with the loving Bacchus reclining in her arms. The god is identified by his pine-cone-tipped staff or 'thyrsus', and by the vine-leaves in his hair. As on the pediment of the

Temple of Bacchus a short distance away, their partnership tells symbolically how the soul of the god's human initiates, redeemed from Hades and oblivion, will celebrate with its deliverer for evermore the eternal triumph and symposium of the blessed. The theme evidently made a profound impression at Pompeii. In the House of the Vettii there is a painting which recalls an earlier stage of the myth: Bacchus, with his healing power of divine love, is seen approaching the sleeping Ariadne. Another fine painting of their story has been discovered in the newly excavated House of Marcus Fabius Rufus; and at a villa outside Stabiae, there is a further notable rendering of the subject.

It was also the theme of elegant stucco reliefs.[12] Later on, in the allegory-loving age of later paganism, many sarcophagi continue to show the same scene, with Ariadne waking to wed Dionysus just as the soul of the initiate will awaken from death to a life of union with the god.

This culminating scene at the Villa of the Mysteries, together with some of the other nine groups of figures on either side, is a copy, how accurate we cannot tell, of an earlier painting. This Greek original had probably decorated the sanctuary of Dionysus at Pergamum (Bergama) in Asia Minor, a place which,

Left: Villa of the Mysteries: *the Pipe Player*
Right: *Dionysus and Ariadne* from the Villa of the Cupid Seller near Stabiae (Castellamare della Stabia)

under the pro-Roman monarchs who ruled there before the Romans annexed their kingdom (133 BC), had boasted a remarkable school of Hellenistic art. In the Pergamum Temple, the centre of the god's mystery cult, this supreme moment of the Sacred Marriage was solemnly re-enacted as the climax of the rites conducted in his honour; and that was the significance of its depiction in the painting. But Pergamum, in its turn, may well have borrowed and adapted the central figures from famous cult images at Smyrna, which was not far away.

The groups on these walls of the Villa of the Mysteries, round the central figures of Bacchus and Ariadne, are vivid, varied, admirably preserved, and often enigmatic. On the central wall itself, the divine pair is flanked by two scenes. A Silenus offers a bowl to a young satyr, while another satyr holds a theatrical mask over the Silenus' head. On the other side, a kneeling woman is about to uncover a shallow basket in order to disclose a phallus, symbol of fecundity, while beyond her a winged, half-naked female figure menacingly raises a long whip.

On the right wall we see the woman who is going to be scourged by this whip. She is cowering, with bared torso, her face buried in the lap of a seated woman who strokes her hair. A nude Bacchant or Maenad moves in an orgiastic dance. Next to her, a woman in bridal yellow, seated on an ivory stool, is arranging her hair, while a Cupid holds a mirror, and another, with his bow, looks on. And finally another woman, with her mantle draped over her head in the manner of a priestess, sits on a chair with a footstool, leaning on a purple and gold cushion.

On the left hand wall a boy, guided by a seated woman, is reading from a papyrus roll, while another boy stands by their side. Then come four women, engaged in a sacrificial rite. Next a fat Silenus plays the lyre, a faun blows his pipe, and his consort is seen suckling a goat. Finally, beyond them a woman is seen whirling round violently, with her hand raised aloft and her drapery tossed about her.[13]

This complex, much-disputed composition appears to depict the rituals, terrors and glories of initiation. We see women, or one woman, performing the

to the divine realm. The mystic bride-to-be is whipped by a terrible deity, for initiation and salvation are not yet hers: those who are not yet fully possessed by Dionysus have to endure his punishment. The chill of horror inspired by this grim scene gives added bliss, by contrast, to the prospective salvation which is displayed in other parts of the picture. Yet the painter has not convinced us, has not tried to convince us, that this happy destiny is unmistakably going to come to ourselves. What his particular talents have achieved instead is a special, peculiar brand of spirituality, a magic, dream-like, shut-in atmosphere, peopled by self-contained 'beings entirely absorbed in their own existence, engrossed in their pursuits and abiding completely unconcerned about us, in a world apart from ours':[14] a world from which no gesture or glance penetrates through to the outside observer.

There were very varying degrees of profundity in ancient expressions of Dionysiac cult. The emotion so successfully expressed by the painter (or rather master-painter, for this large composition was no doubt executed by a whole group), an emotion that was possibly shared by the owners of the house, came at the top of the scale. At the bottom was a much more relaxed sort of feeling. This is parodied by Petronius, who makes the boorish dinner-host Trimalchio dress preparations and suffering the ordeals that give entry

Opposite: This girl is being whipped by a winged demon: part of the initiation rites of Dionysus, as depicted in the Villa of the Mysteries
Right: A detail of the great frieze round three walls of a room in the Villa of the Mysteries: a boy reading

Opposite: Painting from Pompeii showing a couple in pursuit of Bacchic happiness
Below: An attendant of Dionysus, drunken Silenus, on a public fountain in the Via di Nola, Pompeii

up a boy at his dinner-party as Bacchus the Deliverer, Inspirer and Liberator.[15] In the same spirit we find the gardens of Pompeii crammed with little Dionysiac masks and other objects dotted around the foliage or hanging and circulating in the breeze; and painters less serious-minded than the artist of the Villa of the Mysteries show Apollo accompanying the love-play of Bacchus and Ariadne on the lyre.

For this cult, at its least exacting level, tended to succumb to mere sensuality, with the after-life pictured as a sexy debauch; and many were the drinking and dining-clubs that assumed the exalted patronage of Bacchus. At Pompeii this type of materialism was widespread, because, in spite of temples and the occasional exalted artist, the prevalent religious atmosphere was by no means lofty. It can roughly be described as an easy-going Epicureanism, not seeking the austere kind of 'freedom from pain' which the founder Epicurus had pronounced to be his ideal, but strongly inclined to seek pleasure while you can, because tomorrow will be too late – no matter what the mystery religions may say.

That is the significance of a Pompeian mosaic of a skull; and another, from the same place, shows a skeleton holding a cup of wine in each hand. The

One of a pair of silver cups, showing skeletons. Part of the treasure found in the Villa La Pisanella at Boscoreale

skeletons on magnificent silver cups, found at the Villa La Pisanella at nearby Boscoreale, make the same point. 'Enjoy life while you have it,' reads an inscription on one of them, 'for tomorrow is uncertain.' A similar cup in Berlin inscribes a skeleton 'get! and use!'; and yet another skeleton, on a mosaic at the National Museum in Rome, is seen twisting on the funeral pyre and raising itself on its elbow to sneer at the spectator, and warn him: 'Know thyself!' In much later centuries, too, this particular expression of mortal impermanence was by no means disdained even among the devout; for many a Christian church has countless baroque statues of regal or ecclesiastical figures whose magnificent robes only partially conceal the skull that protrudes from beneath.

At Petronius's *Banquet of Trimalchio*,

A slave brought in a silver skeleton, put together in such a way that its joints and backbone could be pulled out and twisted in all directions.

After he had flung it about on the table once or twice, its flexible joints falling into various postures, Trimalchio recited:

Man's life, alas, is but a span,
So let us live it while we can,
We'll be like this when dead![16]

After all, the death-rate was high in the ancient world. As in the majority of countries today, most people never reached the age of forty. The extraordinary array of surgical implements found in the House of the Surgeon at Pompeii shows that doctors did their best, but these probes, catheters and forceps, unaccompanied by anaesthetics, must have failed more often than not to do the trick.

So happiness must be sought for here and now, and the graffiti of Pompeii revert constantly to the words which signify this aim: *felicitas* and *felix*. Another graffitist, however, who stressed the same impermanence, derived from it a message that was optimistic rather than gloomy.

Nothing can last for ever;
Though the sun shines gold
It must plunge into the sea.
The moon has also disappeared
Which but now so brightly gleamed.
If one day thy fair one storms
In wildest fury,
Hold fast, this storm will soon yield
To the soft Zephyr.[17]

The rather low-grade Epicureanism which accompanied the search for pleasure in these Campanian towns was matched by more technical and highbrow manifestations of the same philosophy. In particular, the largest ancient library of papyri that has ever come to light, found in the Villa of the Papyri outside Herculaneum, consists almost entirely of the essays of Epicurean philosophers.

Only a few writings of Epicurus himself have been identified among them. But about two-thirds of the papyri are monographs by Philodemus, who at this period was one of the leaders of Epicureanism in Italy, second only to Virgil's teacher Siro. The headquarters of the movement were at Neapolis and Herculaneum. Philodemus, who came originally from the cultural centre of Gadara near the Sea of Galilee, is evidently the unnamed Epicurean philosopher mentioned by Cicero as a great friend of Lucius Calpurnius Piso Caesoninus, the wealthy father-in-law of Julius Caesar. Philodemus spent much of his time in a villa at Herculaneum,[18] which may well have been given him by Piso. But, if so, this was not the Villa of the Papyri where his manuscripts have been found, for that was much too grand a possession for a Roman nobleman's Greek philosopher friend. Indeed, the mansion may well have belonged to Piso himself, who was a very

likely possessor of this sort of Epicurean library, and has been believed for other reasons to have Herculanean connections. One of Cicero's accusations against him was that he had looted statues from Greece, and the Villa of the Papyri was full of valuable sculpture as well as papyri (Chapter 5). Perhaps it was here that Philodemus lived, as a guest, and not in a villa of his own.

The philosophical works of Philodemus found at Herculaneum, and known only from these finds, are described by Dr Andrew Gow as 'pedestrian in style, earnest in tone, uninspired though not uninteresting in content'. It is therefore curious to come upon a group of lively, amusing and often lecherous Greek poetical epigrams that were also written by a Philodemus. We are told that Cicero's unnamed philosopher was a poet as well, and there is every reason to suppose that they were one and the same person.

Philodemus, then, while his professional treatises adhere to the severe philosophical interpretations offered by his master Epicurus, is closer to local graffiti in his poems – notably this tribute to his mistress Philainion, addressed to the Cyprian goddess Venus.

> She is always ready for
> Anything, and often lets
> Me have it free. I'll put up
> With such a Philainion,
> O golden Cypris, until
> A better one is invented.[19]

And he is free with other comments, too, which illustrate the love-life of Herculaneum or the region round about.

> So I am your 'darling girl'!
> Your tears say so, and the sleights your hands play,
> You are conventionally jealous, and your kisses
> Suggest a lover who knows just what he wants.
> I am the more confused, then.
> For when I whisper 'Here I am, take me, come,'
> You fuss, cough and adjourn the session *sine die*.[20]

Surgical implements found in the House of the Surgeon, Pompeii

Atrium of the Samnite House, Herculaneum (second century BC) with loggia in the Greek (and Renaissance) manner in the upper floor. The panels in the entrance are painted to look like marble, according to the so-called First Style

. Private Houses in Town and Country

The private houses of Pompeii and Herculaneum have been described, with a good deal of justification, as the most wonderful of all the monuments or documents that the ancient world has left behind for our attention. Like houses in Arab countries today, they look inwards, mainly deriving their light not from external windows but from courtyards within. They are refuges of coolness and peace, the realization of a Mediterranean ideal in a hot and noisy environment.

In early days, when they were at their best and most comfortable, these single-storeyed buildings – for that is what, for a long time, they were – expanded liberally over the ground, covering 650 or 750 square metres; and for this reason (although the disappearance of most ancient houses at Rome and elsewhere makes it impossible to dogmatize) they were probably the exception rather than the rule in Italy, where few towns had enough room for lateral expansion.

This original, basic structure possessed an internal symmetry not normally found in the living accommodation of Greece. Such Italian houses, in the words of Professor Frank Brown,

> . . . were tightly organised around the middle space and source of light, in a highly condensed and articulated plan. Its deliberate symmetry and insistent axiality were underscored by the sequence, size, shape and graduated lighting of its members. They were counterbalanced by the attraction of its luminous centre. The clear spatial statement of precedence, the clear shape of before, behind, and beside, and of great and small, both expressed and guided duty, discipline and decorum.[1]

From a broad entrance one entered a sky-lit hall (*atrium*), and passed straight on into a main room called the *tablinum*. Behind this, entered by lateral corridors, there might be a garden, perhaps colonnaded. Though the axial symmetry was sometimes insensitive to siting and layout, no house was ever exactly the same. Each had its own individual physiognomy, and as time went on the variations became more and more strongly marked.

At Pompeii, although traces of earlier residences have been found, the House of the Surgeon is the only identifiable dwelling that seems to precede 200 BC.[2] (The names we use for these buildings today are mostly modern.[3]) Its rectangular plan and simple *atrium* may reflect the designs of prosperous Samnite residences at contemporary towns in the interior, such as Bovianum (Boiano) and Beneventum. But the

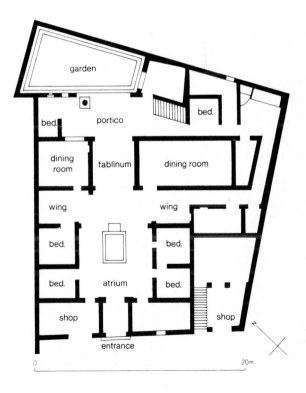

Fig. 6. The House of the Surgeon, Pompeii

great Campanian houses of the second century BC, the Houses of the Faun, Pansa, and Sallust at Pompeii, and the Samnite House at Herculaneum, already belong to a period when these coastal towns had adopted their own pattern. 'And where in our own civilization,' rightly demands Hugh Plommer, 'can we find small provincial towns as elegant as the Pompeii of the tufa period?' The House of Pansa is the most regularly built of these mansions.[4] The House of the Faun, embodying the Greek tastes of the local nobility, is more imposing than any known palace or villa of contemporary Hellenistic kings. And indeed, even if we had such Greek material for comparison, the Pompeian building would still be impressive, with its two *atria*, two colonnaded gardens, and four dining rooms. The interiors are in sober taste, the floors exquisite, and the proportions classical and generous.

And yet spaciousness is not the impression that most visitors carry away from the houses of Pompeii

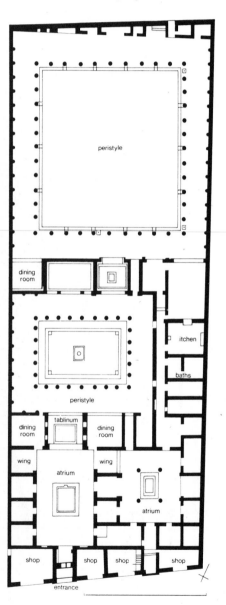

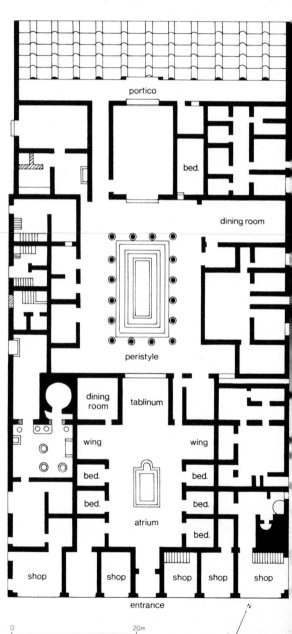

Above: Fig. 7. The House of the Faun, Pompeii
Right: Fig. 8. The House of Pansa, Pompeii

0   20m

in spite of their large overall dimensions. For although the rooms were lofty (at this period they might rise to a height of seven and a half metres), they often seem small and cramped. This particularly struck earlier tourists such as Chateaubriand, who was reminded of doll's houses.

In describing the structure of these buildings it must always be remembered that their interiors were covered with paintings, mosaics and stucco (Chapter 6).

As for the purely architectural features – with which this decoration was inseparably linked – they may be summarized as follows. The houses were entered by a narrow corridor divided by a door into two successive halves, first the *vestibulum*, and then the *fauces*.[5] Next, according to the traditional plan, comes the court or *atrium*, usually with a central opening in its roof, situated over a basin to collect the rain-water.[6] Ancient authorities, Varro and Vitruvius, believed that the *atrium* had originally been the nucleus and

The large, early House of Pansa at Pompeii: looking through the *atrium* to the columned garden court (peristyle) and to Vesuvius behind

principal room of Italian houses and that in early days it had been wholly covered. But there is also a case for taking a different view and supposing that it had initially been the court in front of the house, an open and uncovered space, the shrunken descendant of early Mediterranean courtyards, like that of Tiryns in Greece in the second millennium BC. The problem must be regarded as unsolved. At all events, in historic times the *atrium* possessed a roof, normally with an opening in the centre; and this roof was supported on massive beams of oak and beech. But there were several varieties of *atrium*. At the Houses of the Stags and the Skeleton at Herculaneum, and the House of the Ephebe at Pompeii, the roof was entirely covered in, without any central opening at all. But roofs of this kind were costly to build and maintain; and indeed the same applied to all roofs without columnar supports, so that it began to be quite common to add four or more columns round the tank, after the pattern of a Greek portico. At the Samnite House in Herculaneum the *atrium* has a very singular loggia gallery with columns and semi-columns, the inter-columnar spaces being closed or windowed – a design which looks forward to the Renaissance and goes back to certain Greek proto-types, such as a tomb at Shatby in Egypt (*c.* 260 BC).

Although the *atrium* tended, as time went on, to become little more than a large and richly furnished sitting room, in earlier days its heavy roof and other traditional features had contributed to a general impression of closed-in sanctity. This austere atmos-phere was appropriate to the shrine of the household gods *(lararium)*, which was frequently located in this part of the house. A sort of cupboard, containing the

Fig. 9. Ground Plan of the House of the Tragic Poet at Pompeii

Shrine of the household gods *(lararium)* in the House of Menander at Pompeii

peristyle

dining room

bed.

bed.

kitchen

bed.

tablinum

wing

wing

bed.

bed.

atrium

stairs

stairs

shop

shop

N

entrance

0   20m.

The wooden partition, in the house at Herculaneum named after it. The partition divides off the living room (*tablinum*) from the *atrium*. It had double doors at either end, and in the middle probably a plain expanse of wood (this part was destroyed by eighteenth-century tunnelling). Hinges and lamp-brackets, in the form of ships' prows, have survived

images of the *lares* who were the family's divine ancestors, this shrine was the first thing, we are told by Petronius, to catch the eye in Trimalchio's house; and the comic dramatist Plautus tells how the master's daughter was accustomed to pray there every day, bringing incense and garlands, and wine or some other gift.[7] The *atrium* also contained the treasure chest of the house; and sometimes it was adorned by portrait busts of the owner. At the back, there was traditionally a marble table, the *cartibulum*, a surviving symbol of the ancient household hearth.[8]

On either side of an *atrium*, normally at its far end, were rooms called wings (*alae*), which may originally have contained the images of earlier members of the family. Later, these little chambers were used for a variety of purposes. They also served to let in some additional light through external windows or to provide unobtrusive additional outer doors.

The room known as the *tablinum*, behind the *atrium* in the centre, was closed at the back by a wall containing a door or window. The *tablinum* normally opened along its whole front onto the *atrium*, though wooden partitions or curtains could be added for the sake of privacy. This frontal opening of the room might be crowned with an entablature and flanked by pilasters, rectangular columns which at this position now seem to make their architectural debut, for example in the House of the Faun; another century was to pass before they reached central Italy. According to the theory that the *atrium* was originally a courtyard, the *tablinum* had been the central room of the house (though some Pompeian mansions, such as that of Loreius Tiburtinus, had no *tablinum* at all). Before separate dining-rooms existed, the master and mistress of the house used to eat in the *tablinum*, and used it as reception room, study and bedroom.

Marble table, seen from the side, in the House of Gaius Cornelius Rufus at Pompeii

Even later, the marriage-bed still remained in the *tablinum*, but the actual sleeping accommodation might now be located at a number of different points of the house. The position of beds was often indicated by a special configuration of the floor mosaic, and by a lower, vaulted ceiling, forming a sort of niche. In front of the bedrooms there was sometimes an ante-chamber where a slave spent the night. The sleeping quarters of other slaves had no fixed position, except that the door-keeper might have a small room beside the entrance.

Like the bedrooms of the houses, the dining-room *(triclinium)* could be in a number of different places. Or rather, the dining-rooms in the plural, because the larger houses (like Trimalchio's in the novel of Petronius) had different ones to suit the various seasons; and in the summer people took their meals in the garden, or in a room or arbour adjoining it. Later, as will be seen, the custom arose of dining on an upper storey. On the ground floor, a favourite situation for winter dining-rooms was beside the *tablinum*. In early days Italians had also dined not only in the *tablinum* itself but in the *atrium*, and they began to build special dining rooms only after becoming acquainted with the Greek practice of reclining in order to eat.

Dining-rooms were small, and could only just accommodate the customary three couches even when they were placed against the walls. There was very little space for waiters, or for the slaves men took with them when they dined out as guests. A painting shows a black slave behind a diner; other slaves are to be seen removing his shoes (a necessary measure because of the dirty streets) and offering him wine. The owner of the House of the Moralist inscribed these precepts in white on the black-painted walls of his winter dining-room:[9]

> The slave shall wash and dry the feet of the guests; and let him be sure to spread a linen cloth on the cushions of the couches.
>
> Don't cast lustful glances, or make eyes at another man's wife.
>
> Don't be coarse in your conversation.
>
> Restrain yourself from getting angry or using offensive language. If you can't, go back to your own house.

The room bearing these sage instructions has a vaulted, coffered ceiling. Ceilings, for obvious reasons,

Fig. 10. The House of the Stags

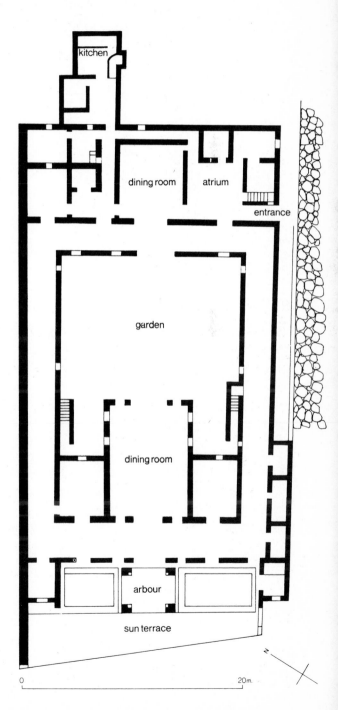

Above: Heating apparatus, Pompeii
Opposite: Relief of a lobster strangely combined with a typical
'sacred landscape' showing the wall of a shrine, possibly
of the god Priapus, to whom an old fisherman dedicates a
lobster in an epigram. Private Collection

are the features of the houses of Pompeii and Herculaneum that have vanished most completely, to the detriment of our ability to imagine what the rooms originally looked like. But their painted, stuccoed, gilded and ivory-inlaid timbers must have contributed greatly to the luxurious appearance of the houses – and to their claustrophobic atmosphere as well.

Kitchen arrangements were makeshift and cramped. Even if the Roman expression for a whole meal is 'from eggs to apples', once cooking had become an art in the second century BC many people started doing themselves pretty well. A cook cost the price of a horse, and by the time of the Plinies three horses was nearer the mark (though he was still only worth a third as much as a really expensive fish). Earlier generations had done their simple cooking almost anywhere, perhaps in the *atrium* or out in the open. But even at a later date houses had no fixed position for the kitchen; it was put wherever a little free space could be found. The kitchens at Pompeii were poky little holes, with scarcely room for more than one slave. Such space as could be found was largely occupied by a sink and a brick oven on a raised hearth, perhaps supplemented by a smaller oven for baking bread, with the addition of a bronze heating apparatus. There were no chimneys, and the only escape for the smoke was through a window or a hole in the roof – an arrangement, or lack of one, which was responsible for a great many fires.[10] The ovens burnt wood or charcoal; they remained virtually unchanged in rural Italy until the recent introduction of bottled gas (which has meant an increase in the consumption of fried food).

In the absence of fireplaces, charcoal-burning braziers were employed to heat the houses at Pompeii and Herculaneum. Heating presented a severe problem. For it can be perishingly cold at these places, with a strong wind coming from the north-east; one wonders, looking at houses of such a kind, whether the winter climate must not have been at least a little warmer in antiquity. A more or less translucent substance, *lapis specularis*, was sometimes used to cover windows, occasionally in private houses, but mainly in public places such as baths.

This material is sometimes described as talc or mica, but it appears to have been selenite, a crystallized or foliated form of gypsum or sulphate of lime, which

Perseus with the head of the gorgon Medusa: a painting from Pompeii

was often found in the form of thin plates and was still used to glaze windows as late as the eighteenth century. However, a kind of coarse glass was also known; it was rather like the soda-lime glass sometimes used for making bottles of soft drinks today. Glass was employed in certain rooms of the grander sort of house,[11] for example in bathrooms and bedroom alcoves (as well as sedan chairs); and the Central Baths at Pompeii and the Suburban Baths at Herculaneum can still show glass panes. Normally about six millimetres thick, the panes were inserted in the wall or in a bronze or wood sash, which turned vertically round a pivot. Because of the costliness of these panes, it was felt necessary to protect them by curtains, blinds, wooden shutters or nets.[12] Later on, in Gaul and Britain, it was found essential to make much more extensive use of glass for private residences, if people were to avoid freezing to death;[13] but at Pompeii and Herculaneum its employment had been the exception rather than the rule.

The alternatives, such as the practice of hanging cloths or skins over the windows and skylights, provided inadequate shelter, and they got drenched by the rain. The only other thing that could be done was to close up the window completely by shutters, which either folded or slid into the wall, as was the case in the dining-room of the House of the Moralist. The younger Pliny liked keeping his shutters closed at the beginning of the day, because the total blackness helped him to think.[14] Besides, at certain seasons of the year, either you barricaded yourself up in the pitch dark or you got exceedingly cold, and hermetically sealed bedrooms became very stuffy; although the smell was sometimes disguised by burning bread.

Even so it was chilly in the winter; and the stone floors must have been unwelcoming to bare feet in sandals. It was unfortunate if, like Augustus, one felt the cold badly. He used to wear four tunics over his toga; and then on top of them he put on a cloak, or even two.

The blocked up windows only intensified what was already a very serious problem, the lighting of the houses. Even in the most luxurious mansions this was very inadequate. The Romans knew of crude oil or petroleum, but it was so inflammable that nobody made use of it. Instead they employed torches, or tapers, or candles made of tallow fat rolled round a twisted wick. Or rather, the rich used these candles, because the poor, even if they had been able to pay for them, would have been tempted to eat the fat. The wicks could be placed inside lanterns, stationary or portable, in which the light was protected by semi-transparent sides of horn or bladder or (at a later date) glass. But excavations at Pompeii and Herculaneum have also yielded an enormous abundance of lamps of every size, shape and degree of luxury, made of bronze as well as terracotta. And at the House of the Wooden Partition at Herculaneum, for example, the uprights of the partition itself carried bronze attachments in the form of figure-heads of ships, on which lamps could be hung at night.

However, a lamp consisting of a single candle gives only one-hundredth as much light as a sixty-watt electric bulb. A splendid candelabrum with fourteen wicks could illuminate a banquet, but few people could afford to have one. And even when they did, the smoke and smell of the tapers must have spread a thick and oily pall over a Roman feast. Reading, too, was very difficult in such conditions. There are many references to eye troubles due to ocular strain and dirt-infection; ophthalmic remedies were in great demand. The bad lighting, combined with the absence of spectacles, meant that most people stopped being able to read very much at quite an early age. The gentry depended for their reading and writing on trusted slaves.

So, from our point of view, these houses provided a curious mixture of gracious and ungracious living.

The water-supply, on the whole – though we might not have liked certain aspects of it – came on the credit side of the balance. At least, it was far in advance of what is found beside many Mediterranean coasts today. In spite of the strong ancient taste for bathing in communal establishments, many of the large town houses and country villas had private bathing installations of their own; [15] and even their humbler retainers and slaves could get daily hot baths. All houses, except the poorest, had water-pipes fitted with taps – though running water was not to be expected in bedrooms; even in the very grand Villa of Diomede the room where the master slept included an alcove equipped with a table and basin, which was no doubt provided with water from a jug. But in the Villa of the Papyri outside Herculaneum, the garden fountains were supplied by a remarkable system of hydraulic pipes. In early days, a big house had depended on its own wells. At Pompeii two of these, dating back to the early third century BC, have been found beneath the House of the Faun.

The ancient Italians were addicted to public lavatories as well as public baths, but the houses at Pompeii and Herculaneum naturally had their own private lavatories as well. One of these, in the House of the Gem at Herculaneum, contains a graffito of the very last days of the town, conveying the good news that 'Apollinaris the physician of the emperor Titus had a good shit here.' Private houses did not normally possess the facilities of the Forum Baths in the same town, where the toilet could be flushed with water flowing from the cold plunge. But at the House of the Neptune Mosaic there was a pipe down to a sewer; and elsewhere, the pipes led down, if not to a sewer, at least to a trench. Often the lavatory, like the bath-room, was unhygienically close to the kitchen, but at the House of Amandus at Pompeii it is in the dark angle below the flight of stairs. One has the impression that there was a certain shortage of latrine accommodation, for graffiti insistently warn against defecating in the street against house-walls and tombs – sometimes adding, in crude terms, that the practice is inadvisable, owing to the presence of stinging nettles. Indeed, even hotels sometimes lacked not only sufficient lavatories but chamber-pots, to judge by a verse a visitor has scrawled up in his room:

My host, I've wet the bed. My sins I bare.
But why? you ask. No pot was anywhere. [16]

It is time to get away to the subject of gardens. As Shelley observed, 'unlike the inhabitants of the Cimmerian ravines of modern cities, the ancient Pompeians could contemplate the clouds and lamps of heaven.'

It is impossible to say when gardening first came to these towns. The antique House of the Surgeon already had a small garden, and elsewhere, even in the earliest times, there may well have been kitchen-plots behind the domestic buildings. But in the second century BC, if not before, these mansions began to incorporate garden courts or peristyles. Such courts, reached by passages round the *tablinum*, were flanked with colonnades, sometimes two-storeyed, [17] which ran round one or more sides, or every side, of the open space. These side-walks, pent-housed like the cloisters of a small monastery, were adjoined by airy flanking rooms, rectangular or apsed. Colonnaded courts of such a kind, with basins or fountains as their centre-pieces, had been a Greek fashion since after the time of Alexander the Great (who died in 323 BC). But the peristyles we know of at Hellenistic Olynthus in Macedonia and Priene in western Asia Minor, as well as on the island of Delos in the Aegean, had been paved with mosaics, whereas at Pompeii they were habitually filled by a garden. What forerunners Pompeian peristyles may have had in Italy we cannot tell, but the idea had been exported from Greece at quite an early date to this Campanian coast, where the Hellenistic taste for colonnades and porticoes was adapted to Italian needs. Some rich residences of the Vesuvian cities had two, or even more, of these colonnaded peristyles; in the House of the Citharist or Lyre-Player there were rooms which enjoyed a vista of no less than three such courts with different ground-levels.

They enabled the relatively dark and stuffy rooms to remain in continual touch with the fresh air; and in due course the inhabited centres of many mansions were gradually transplanted from the traditional front rooms to the greater space and privacy of the chambers and alcoves looking out upon these garden-courts at the back, leaving the frontal, *atrium*, section as a comparatively unused and largely formal relic of earlier times. The House of the Silver Wedding at Pompeii presents a strong contrast between dark *atrium* and sun-lit peristyle. But the best preserved peristyle today is the garden retreat of the House of the Vettii, an early building restored by wealthy business men, Aulus Vettius Restitutus and Aulus Vettius Conviva, towards the end of the town's life.

Sometimes, too, the garden broke right outside the bounds of the colonnaded courtyard. Behind the Villa of Julia Felix, for example – the largest Pompeian residence yet discovered – there is an extensive piece of ground, containing a fishpond, vegetable garden and orchard.[18] At the House of Loreius Tiburtinus, the

The garden of the Villa of Julia Felix, Pompeii. Along its length ran a fish-pond crossed by miniature marble bridges, and interspersed with grottoes and little shrines

central feature of the big garden is a T-shaped fish pool, with the longer arm flowing down a vine-covered terrace onto a lower level. Along the length of the pool is a profusion of pergolas, grottoes, chapels, fountains and miniature cascades, fore-shadowing, on a small scale, great Renaissance water-gardens like the Villa d'Este at Tibur (Tivoli) – the town from which, by a coincidence, Loreius originated. A wall in his garden displays holes into which the roof of a shed was once fitted, for the protection of exotic plants and blooms. The trees which stood in the garden can still be identified today from the imprints of the roots left in the lava, and now the same varieties have been planted once again: pears, figs, pomegranates and chestnuts. In recent years the men in charge of the sites of Pompeii and Herculaneum have everywhere taken great care to plant only the trees, shrubs, and flowers which on analysis of the rubble and on inspection of ancient paintings prove to have grown there in antiquity. Faithful to the past, too, are the roses, violets and hyacinths in the peristyle of the House of the Vettii.

The people of Pompeii and Herculaneum evidently agreed with the Roman view that gardening is a rewarding, life-enhancing occupation. Indeed, ac-

Above: Shrine-like fountain in the garden of the House of Loreius Tiburtinus, Pompeii
Opposite: The garden (peristyle) of the House of the Vettii at Pompeii. The identity of the ancient plants was deduced from the holes left by their roots

Fig. 11. The House of the Vettii, Pompeii

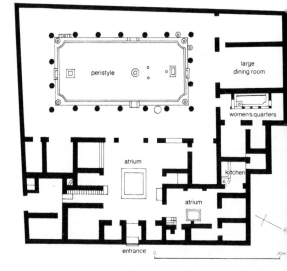

uaintance with the gardens of Campania no doubt helped to stimulate this view among the Romans, though it was already ingrained in their minds, since they had always been deeply attached to the country-ide. In early days, flowers were customarily included n many a kitchen-garden, and later on they were mported to Rome in masses from Tusculum (Frascati) nd Praeneste (Palestrina). Then, in the second entury BC, Greek horticultural experts began to rrive in central Italy and created Roman pleasure ;ardens on the estates of the younger Scipio Africanus nd Decimus Junius Brutus the Augur. In the ollowing century, however, these early attempts were clipsed by the great parks of Pompey and Lucullus.

The luxury of water and plants was rated very highly ndeed, and this passion explains a great deal in Roman rchitecture and art. Gardens were also recognized s terrestrial symbols of the paradise that the religion f Bacchus promised every initiate (Chapter 4). This eing so, they were crammed, especially from the time f Nero onwards, with Dionysiac reliefs, statues, and nasks or discs oscillating in the wind. Even in their :ss successful manifestations these ornaments, aug-nented by grottoes and sundials, rise well above the lastic gnomes of modern gardens. At their best they val, beneath the summer sun, the blend of nature and art effected by gardeners of the Italian Renaissance. Birds, too, were very popular, and an aviary was an important part of every substantial garden.

Moreover, Pompeii and Herculaneum clearly show that the poor felt the same love of cultivated nature and flowers as the rich. Some houses, which are too small to own a single peristyle or even a tree, never-theless have a garden; to make it look larger, a horticultural scene, with Dionysiac adjuncts, is very likely to be painted on its back wall. The people who lived behind shops often had charming little gardens of their own. Or, even if they had not, they placed their windows so as to enjoy the view of a neighbour's greenery. And, as today, there were window-boxes, and vine pergolas abounded on balconies. Vegetables, too, gave aesthetic satisfaction, as Virgil's *Georgics* show; and the same feeling is present in this verse of Herculaneum's adopted poet, Philodemus.

Roses are already here,
Sosylos, and fresh peas,
And the first cut sprouts, and
The minnows that taste of
The surf, and salt soft cheese,
And the tender leaves of
Crinkly lettuces . . .[19]

The colonnade of the Villa of the Marine Gate at Pompeii beneath the approach to the gate, which is seen top right. The villa was partially uncovered by the bombing in 1944

On the southern flanks of Pompeii and Herculaneum, where the spurs of lava descended sharply, marked deviations from traditional house-design occurred, and terraced dwellings were built to exploit the lie of the land. Mention has already been made of two residences in this quarter of Pompeii, belonging to Loreius Tiburtinus and Julia Felix, and at the southwestern extremity of the town the Villa of the Marine Gate was built on two levels to provide vaulted spaces in which the occupants could take shelter from the summer. Against the town-wall stands a colonnade of forty-three columns, which was revealed by bombing in 1944; and so was the dining-room. But this elaborate dwelling, half town-house and half country-house, had already been destroyed twice before that occasion, because it suffered severe damage in the earthquake of AD 62 and had still not been completely reconstructed when final ruin descended in 79.

In Herculaneum, too, the existence of a sharp cliff at the south-western extremity of the town encouraged the abandonment of the traditional Pompeian type of house in favour of a more Mediterranean configuration. A whole row of mansions at this point displays groups of climbing, superimposed terraces, equipped with verandas, loggias and pergolas, and windowed bays and open porticoes looking out over the sea. The House of the Hotel is crowned by a terrace which probably enjoyed the finest view in Herculaneum. The House of the Mosaic Atrium is dominated by a large colonnaded garden, adjoining a dining-room which looks out towards the south-west across a sun-terrace. But the richest of all these southward-facing mansions is the House of the Stags, where the colonnade is replaced by a windowed corridor of modern appearance; and above the terrace rises a four-pilastered pergola with terracotta vases of flowers. Another elegant dwelling, the House of the Gem, is almost swallowed up by the House of the Relief of Telephus, which possesses, in one of its rooms, the most sumptuous marble decoration of floor and wall which has survived from any private abode. This whole elaborately designed mansion makes brilliant use of the uneven terrain, incorporating a whole series of ramps and staircases, some leading to levels that have not yet been fully uncovered.

Staircases were, of course, nothing new at Pompeii and Herculaneum. It is true that the oldest houses, with their liberally spreading extension over the ground, had essentially been one-storey affairs. Indeed, the *atrium* with its partly open roof, and the *tablinum* with its gable, were by no means conducive to vertical development. Nevertheless, attempts to expand upwards soon followed. But they were made in piecemeal fashion, at different heights and with a multiplicity of staircases, which were inserted unobtrusively without any overall plan. The earliest upper rooms in Rome were used as additional dining-rooms *(cenacula)* – often surmounted by a terrace – and Cicero describes how fashionable they were becoming. And similar developments occurred at Pompeii and Herculaneum, for example in the House of the Wooden Partition at the latter town, where an additional storey was boldly added to the original structure. Water-pipes could be carried with rising mains to these upper floors, and a few houses had pipes descending from upstairs lavatories.

These vertical additions continued to be regarded as insignificant from the point of view of architectural design. Nevertheless, experiments in this direction continued, for in the later Republic, in Rome and elsewhere, the combined factors of rising population, rapid industrialization and increased ground rents caused a revolution in constructional methods. In the capital, these factors stimulated the erection of higher and higher buildings. Concrete often made this a practical proposition (Chapter 3), but when the job was done on the cheap (as was the case with certain houses owned by Cicero)[20] the results were dangerously rickety. Pompeii and Herculaneum, where the problems were less severe, lagged well behind these developments. All the same, even there, from the first century BC onwards, the transformation of *atrium* houses into two- or even three-storeyed buildings began to be speeded up. Lit by windows in the outer walls, the upper rooms often had continuous open colonnades, pent-house-roofed loggias and light, projecting balconies carried on wooden piers.

During the first century AD this vertical urge was accentuated by a strong tendency for the large old houses to be split up. It had long been the practice for portions of them to be let off to shops (Chapter 7), and now this was done more and more, and, in addition, the mansions themselves were divided into a number of separate middle-class apartments.[21] At Herculaneum, for example, where this process of subdivision got under way particularly quickly – perhaps under the influence of social changes further along the coast – the House of the Hotel was clumsily fragmented into a series of independent lodgings. These developments intensified the tendency towards verticality, because the new apartments, having so much less ground space than the old residences which they carved up, found it necessary to find compensatory space upstairs. Furthermore, an attempt was made to meet this new situation by embarking on entirely new technical processes. The most remarkable example so far to be discovered is the Trellis House at Herculaneum, built lightly and inexpensively of wood and plaster (Chapter 3). Its *atrium* is replaced by a 'modern' sort of open inner court, a phenomenon also found in the House of the Beautiful Courtyard. These spaces furnished light, air and water, and were flanked by an external stair to an upper storey. In the Trellis House this upper floor, which is excellently preserved (in one room the furnishings were found complete), has a projecting, roofed and balustraded loggia which is propped on brick pillars and overhangs the whole width of the pavement. The house was designed for occupation by two families, one downstairs and one upstairs. They shared nothing but the cistern; the rope to draw the water, and the

Opposite: The House of the Beautiful Courtyard, Herculaneum. A court, with staircase to the upper floor, has replaced the traditional *atrium*
Below: The Trellis House, belonging to the last days of Herculaneum. A family lived on each floor, and this enclosed inner courtyard provided light, ventilation and water for both apartments

windlass, are still to be seen, only slightly scorched by the eruption.

The old-fashioned *atrium* houses of Pompeii and Herculaneum, which such buildings tended to replace, are much less typical of Italian life as a whole than the great tenement blocks of apartment houses constructed at Rome. These are known to us not so much from the capital itself, where only fragmentary examples have survived, as from its port Ostia, where they superseded houses of Pompeian type[22] and have been preserved on an impressive scale. In the capital, we are told, under the influence of Nero's urbanistic ideals and reforms, Roman tenements at last began to assume more durable shape. As regards the coastal towns of Campania, probably the new formulas came first of all to Neapolis and Puteoli, and were just beginning to reach the towns closer to Vesuvius at the time when these were destroyed. In the Via del Foro at Pompeii a new block of this kind had been constructed, and at Herculaneum the Apartment House near the Palaestra was a mature example of the same sort of building, with a massive frontage and a height that we can only guess at from the twelve-metre-high walls that have survived. That would have been the pattern of the future.

The exteriors of the houses of Pompeii and Herculaneum cannot have looked at all as they do today. The roofs, mostly flat though sometimes sloped, were covered by tiles of bright red and yellow terracotta, and house-fronts were vividly painted in accordance with what may have been common practice in antiquity. At first, it is true, the old mansions of Sarnus limestone had presented a simpler and more austere external appearance. But subsequently façades were faced with stucco, sometimes including decorative reliefs, and their lower sections, at least, were covered with a wide variety of paintings. At houses in the southern area of Pompeii the brilliance of the sunlight inspired a preference for giving the exteriors a black ground, displaying figures painted mainly in white.

The brick half-columns flanking the house doors were likewise stuccoed and painted. The 'Pompeian red' is still visible at the House of the Grand Portal at Herculaneum, named after a fine door of a type reproduced again and again in the Renaissance and eighteenth century. Doorways at Pompeii and Herculaneum show a great variety of different shapes and designs, plain or decorated, with or without

Opposite: The door of the House of the Great Portal, Herculaneum; an architectural form much imitated in the Renaissance. To the right is the sports ground (Palaestra)
Below: The door of the House of the Faun at Pompeii. The The greeting *have* (*ave*) is on the threshold

Capitals of this type, showing Dionysiac scenes or
reliefs of husband and wife, adorned the doors of the early
Samnite houses. Pompeii Museum

porches and outside benches. The big 'Samnite'
Republican houses had entrances adorned with
capitals displaying Dionysiac and conjugal scenes. By
the House of Loreius Tiburtinus at Pompeii a
bronze gate, surmounted by a laurel wreath in stone,
still partially survives. The leaves of these doors were
not attached to the doorposts by hinges, but turned
on wooden pivots coated with iron or bronze. At the
House of the Bull there was a double entrance, making
it possible to go in by a little side-door without
exposing the interior to view.

Exteriors were virtually without windows: at the
most there were a few small ones – for example in the
wings of the *atrium*. With such minor exceptions, it
was considered preferable to provide all light from
the inside, because security was a major problem. The
elder Pliny writing about Rome, refers to 'the vast
number of shocking burglaries', in the absence of
an effective police force; and no doubt a similar
problem made itself felt in the Italian towns. At
Pompeii and Herculaneum the solutions were blank
outside walls and bolted doors, supplemented no
doubt by vigilant doorkeepers and by the fierce
dogs whom we see represented on mosaics at the
entrances, inscribed 'Beware of the Dog' *(Cave
canem)*.

On the slopes of Vesuvius outside the gates of Pompeii and Herculaneum, as well as along the coast and in all the countryside around, there were mansions, some of them very large. To distinguish them from town-houses we have to use the ancient term 'villa', though in the English of today it conveys a more pedestrian impression. These residences were not inhabited by their rich owners all the year round; and they were frequently combined with farms. The geographer Strabo, writing early in the first century A D, described the Bay of Naples as an unbroken series of towns, residences and plantations – one continuous city.²³ And the elder Pliny, like Boccaccio thirteen hundred years later, commented how 'extremely thick upon that beautiful coast' the villas clustered. The Bay of Paestum or Gulf of Salerno, further to the south, likewise had its full share.

The villas in these zones which have been noted and examined, or in a few cases excavated, were estimated in 1931 to be thirty-nine in number, and a very great many more could be added now. Some of them date back at least to the second century BC; but new mansions continued to be built for more than a hundred years after that. In the earthquake of AD 62 some of these complexes of buildings were too badly damaged for subsequent repair to be practicable. But on the whole they stood up to the tremors better than the more cramped houses in the towns. Remembering that this had been so, some people took refuge out here in the country during the eruption of 79, although, in fact, villas and refugees alike were rapidly and completely obliterated.

In the first century BC many Romans had taken the waters of Pompeii for curative purposes, just as they took the waters of Puteoli; and Herculaneum was a place of fashion, almost as smart as Cumae or Baiae at the other end of the bay. Cicero had a moderate sized villa at Pompeii for the last twenty years of his life, and liked it because people did not bother him there. Augustus's grandson Agrippa Postumus owned a villa, perhaps built by his father Agrippa, at the place now called Boscotrecase, which, together with its neighbour Boscoreale, formed a great centre for such houses and farms a kilometre or two north of Pompeii. Postumus' sister the elder Agrippina, the wife of Germanicus, was banished for a time to a villa at Herculaneum, which her son Caligula subsequently destroyed, thus abolishing a navigator's landmark. Then, in the reign of Nero, the novelist Petronius

Head of a young man wearing the cloak and veil of a priest: perhaps a member of the Imperial family such as Agrippa Postumus or Marcellus. Pompeii Museum

endows his burlesque hero Trimalchio with a Pompeian property: but such was Trimalchio's great wealth that it completely slipped his mind.[24]

The general appearance of these country residences can be seen from a number of local paintings. The great colonnaded porticoes and façades that they depict seem reminiscent of earlier buildings in Greece, such as the Leonidaeum erected at Olympia in the fourth century BC; yet the villa remained a distinctive Italian invention. And these country-houses round the Bays of Naples and Salerno were fundamentally different from the town mansions of Pompeii and Herculaneum, other than those on the southern terraces of the two places. The rural villas, it is true, looked inwards like their urban counterparts, fronting

an *atrium* or, more frequently, a large peristyle round which the rooms were more or less casually grouped. But the difference from the town houses lay in the fact that the country residences were planned to look outwards as well. They were located and designed, in order to derive the maximum benefit from their superb landscape and climate: and this involved the virtual abolition of their outside walls. In this sense, then, these seaside and hillside palaces were at one with the countryside. But in another sense they were quite external to it, being situated on a series of artificial platforms in the middle of large estates. These surrounding hectares consisted of parklands in which laurels, planes and pines, and clusters of exotic shrubs, alternated with formal beds of clipped myrtles and flowers.

A little way outside the Herculaneum Gate stood the dignified Villa of Diomede. Excavated during the years 1771–4, when the discovery of eighteen skeletons in the cellar created a sensation, the building was stripped of its fine paintings, which are now in the Naples Museum. The colonnaded entrance leads straight into the peristyle, an arrangement which, according to Vitruvius, is appropriate for a country villa (though in fact there are two main types, often merging, the peristyle villa and the more elongated type of portico villa). The south side of the peristyle is flanked by an apsed sunroom, and a lower level is adorned by the largest garden in the whole Pompeian region. Its trees, shrubs and flowers, grouped round a fountain, fish-pond and pergola (used as a summer dining-room), stood within a continuous colonnade. To the stroller within its shade, the space between each pilaster framed a different, delightful picture of land and sea; and the terraced belvederes at the corners of the walk, facing the coast, enjoy one of the most agreeable vistas in the world.

A little further out from Pompeii stands the most splendid of all these country mansions, the Villa of the Mysteries (Villa Item). Here is the room filled with remarkable murals illustrating the mystic cult of Bacchus (Chapter 4). When excavations began in 1909, they had to penetrate beneath seven and a half metres of volcanic earth, and there was peril from poisonous gases. But in 1929 and 1930 the work continued and restoration proceeded, though the site has still not been completely cleared today. Built on a seaward slope, the Villa of the Mysteries was in use for three centuries, starting with more or less the shape of a large early town house and developing lavishly into

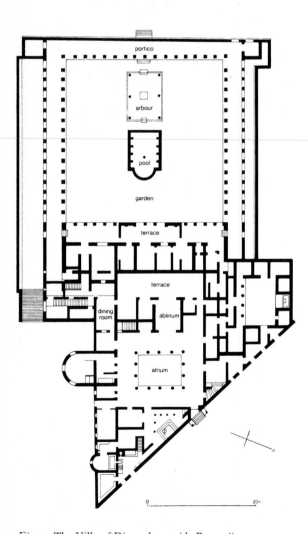

Fig. 12. The Villa of Diomede outside Pompeii

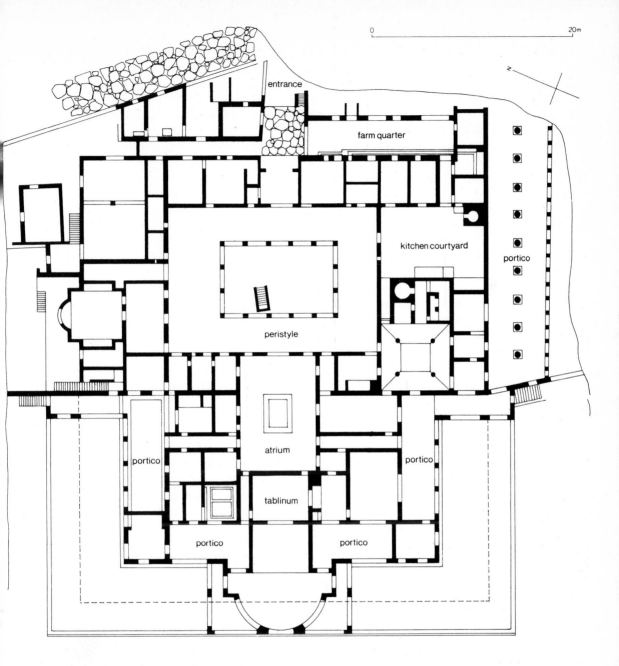

0   20m

Fig. 13. The Villa of the Mysteries outside Pompeii

a country villa of sixty rooms. The original entrance on the east side led straight through a short passage into a peristyle, round which the main living-rooms are grouped; and the whole extensive area facing south, east and west, raised high above subterranean vaults, is rich with broad, splendid, hanging gardens.

The discovery of a statue of Livia, the wife of Augustus, has aroused speculations whether the Villa of the Mysteries may not have been an imperial property. But this does not, of course, necessarily follow from the presence of the statue, though the owners were clearly men of some importance.

Inscriptions suggest that one of them may have been a member of the Samnite noble family of the Istacidii, who possess a fine mausoleum nearby. After the earthquake of AD 62 had inflicted serious damage, the villa appears, to judge by a seal found in the slaves' quarters, to have passed into the hands of a freedman of the former owners, a certain Lucius Istacidius Zosimus. He may have been the man who now proceeded to wall up certain old doorways and cut new ones, leaving the earlier master's quarters empty and converting the place into a large-scale farm.[25] A further owner of the same period is mocked by a caricature of a laureate head scratched on the wall and inscribed: 'This is Rufus.'[26]

Another area much favoured for country mansions was the maritime hillside above Stabiae (Castellamare di Stabia), some five kilometres south of Pompeii, the place where the elder Pliny went to rescue his friend Pomponianus and met his death on the beach (Chapter 2). At least twelve villas, varying from palatial residences to farms, have been identified in the area. Casual digging on Varano (Barano) hill took place between 1749 and 1782, and the objects discovered are now to be seen at Naples. From 1950 onwards and again in the 1960s, excavations have been renewed, and large villas are now uncovered. Of the important paintings found on their walls some remain on the spot and others have been taken to the Antiquarium at Castellamare di Stabia. The Villa of the Cupid Seller (Villa della Venditrice di Amori)[27] is aligned with the face of the hillside. Its extensive open colonnaded terrace was fitted with large windows enjoying a fine

panorama of the Bay of Naples and the coastal mountains, while the dining-room looks out over Vesuvius. A room behind contains grotesque graffiti of a gladiator fight. Another exceptionally splendid mansion, the Villa of Obsidian Vases [28] (subjected to destructive digging in the eighteenth century), has recently been discovered to possess three main units, at different levels. One of these units is centred round a peristyle with spiral columns; a second set of rooms is grouped about another large colonnaded area containing a twenty-seven metre-long swimming pool in the middle of a garden which faces onto the sea and, as the casts of tree-roots show, was once surrounded by planes. And, finally, a further range of apartments flanks a four-columned *atrium*. And this villa, too, contains its graffiti – on the walls of the adjoining farm quarters.[29]

Boscoreale and Boscotrecase, on the other side of Pompeii, were likewise full of country houses (though it is not easy to get an idea of them now). The medieval names of the two places were Nemus Scyphati and Silva Mala respectively, and Boscoreale became the game forest of monarchs. In ancient times, one villa at Boscotrecase, as we saw, belonged to a member of the imperial family, Agrippa Postumus, and two others at Boscoreale have yielded, respectively, the finest architectural paintings that have come down to us (Villa of Publius Fannius Sinistor or Lucius Herennius Florus, Chapter 6), and one of the most important of all silver treasures (Villa La Pisanella). Yet these two estates, like many others, were as much concerned with farming as with private luxury, possessing not

These views of country houses on paintings from Pompeii give some idea of what mansions such as the Villa of the Papyri looked like. Naples Museum

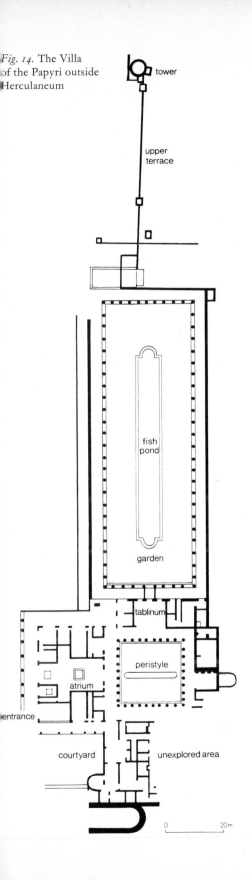

Fig. 14. The Villa of the Papyri outside Herculaneum

tower

upper terrace

fish pond

garden

tablinum

peristyle

atrium

entrance

courtyard

unexplored area

0   20m

only elegant residential quarters, but also agricultural sections which are too extensive and professional to be regarded as merely the farming adjuncts sometimes added to such palaces as contributions to upkeep and to the owner's pride. Something will be said of the farms of the area when the material resources of Pompeii are discussed (Chapter 7).

But the most lavishly endowed country mansion of all is the Villa of the Papyri, on the slope of Vesuvius, just outside the western end of Herculaneum, where it covers an area of 33,465 (245 × 137) square metres. After the area had been buried under a fresh stratum of lava in 1631, digging operations between 1738 and 1765 disclosed a fabulous collection of statues and papyri. But thereafter all the tunnels and vents were closed, and the site was abandoned – with an alacrity stimulated by the poisonous vapours that emanated from its depths. Fortunately, however, a plan of the lay-out, in so far as this had become known, still remained; it had been drawn up by the engineer Karl Weber, the only man at that time who had any real idea how an excavation should be carried out. The original house itself was a low building with a small *atrium* – hardly more than an entrance hall – and a large peristyle flanked by a *tablinum* commanding a wide view. But beyond the *tablinum* the people who owned the villa during the first century BC added another huge, oblong, colonnaded terrace-park, extending to the north-west. It contained a large pool and terminated, just above the sea, in a round tower or belvedere, decorated with a sumptuous marble pavement.[30] Below lay a beach with a private harbour and boat-houses, and this was the point now chosen for the main entrance, which was marked by an impressive columned portico.

The statuary found in this residence and garden can be seen in the Naples Museum. It comprises many marble sculptures, and the greatest single collection of ancient bronzes that has ever come to light. Altogether ninety pieces were discovered, ranging all the way from the archaic period to the first century BC. Some are originals, others copies by skilful and sometimes masterly hands. The bronzes include eighteen statues of various sizes, and thirty-two portrait busts. In marble, there are seven statues and fifteen heads: these portraits, in bronze and marble alike, represent a wide range of people – Greek monarchs, generals, orators, thinkers, personages of the theatre. Many of the objects in this collection were found in the *tablinum;* and the large porticoed garden, too, was a gallery of works of art, arranged between the columns, and among the trees and the plants, and on the edges of the pool. Eighteenth-century archaeologists all over the western world were deeply impressed when this collection came to light – artists somewhat less so, since with the exception of a fine 'Hermes in Repose' they did not feel that any of the finds improved upon what they already knew from Rome.

The other sensational discovery consisted of huge numbers of papyri. The tunnel bored by the early excavators eventually opened up a room with a fine marble floor. And this, it turned out, adjoined a smaller room lined with wooden shelves, which survived in a carbonized condition. On these shelves lay numerous objects which appeared to be small black bricks; others were found on two sides of an additional set of shelves in the middle of the room. But the bricks turned out to be papyrus rolls, each carbonized inside its wooden case. This was the first ancient library that had ever been found, for no one then dreamt of the wealth hidden in the sands of Egypt, which have subsequently yielded so, many more papyri than any other country. In the early attempts to unroll and decipher the finds in the Villa of the Papyri, very many of the rolls were destroyed. By 1806, however, the number of those deciphered had reached a total of ninety-six. In the early 1820s, the British envoy to Naples, Sir William A'Court, obtained eighteen in exchange for the same number of kangaroos, sent to King Ferdinand IV for his zoological garden. Half a century later, 341 papyri had been unrolled and 195 published, and the number preserved, complete or in fragmentary condition, was estimated at 1,803. Of these, 800 scrolls still remain to be read in the National Library at Naples; and a few are to be seen in the National Archaeological Museum.

It is indeed remarkable, after the violent fate which overtook Herculaneum and the villa, that it was possible to decipher any of the papyri at all. Yet, after the circumstances of their burial had given them the appearance and consistency of carbon, the fragile fibrous material still preserved the marks of the writing; and in cases where the highly delicate task of prising the leaves apart does prove to be practicable, the opaque black of the letters, written in excellent ink, can be distinguished from the clear blackness of the background. But, even so, there remain grave problems. The papyri, says Oswyn Murray, 'are extremely brittle. Only the shine of the ink (which easily vanishes) as the papyrus is tilted back and forth in different lights, or (where the surface has gone) the marks in the underlying fibres, are visible. Where the evidence has disappeared, reliance must be placed on the copy made about the time of unrolling, usually by a man with little Greek whose chief skill was draughtsmanship.'[31]

For the works have nearly all turned out to be Greek – less than two dozen are in Latin, one being a fragment of a poem on Augustus' victory over Antony and Cleopatra at the Battle of Actium. As was mentioned in Chapter 4, the papyri are nearly all Epicurean treatises, with an overwhelming emphasis on the works of a contemporary exponent of that philosophy, Philodemus, so that it has been supposed that this great villa belonged to his friend and patron Lucius Calpurnius Piso Caesoninus, the father-in-law of Julius Caesar.

Seeing that casual, inexpert investigation revealed this remarkable library, and uncovered a no less extraordinary collection of statues as well, it is very likely that excavation by modern methods, if this could ever by undertaken in the Villa of the Papyri, would be able to claim equally outstanding finds. And this was only one of many Italian country mansions. Often they were grander still: Horace complains of these impudent magnates, who were encroaching upon what belonged to the sea.

The fishes feel the ocean narrowing
From all the rubble thrown into the deep,
And still contractors and their workmen fling
Cement to it, for one who cannot keep
To solid earth.[32]

Bronze statue of seated Hermes (Mercury), based on an original by Lysippus (fourth century BC). One of the most admired among the pieces of sculpture found in the Villa of the Papyri

6. Paintings, mosaics and furniture

The architectural features of the houses, it must be repeated, have to be considered in the closest possible relationship to the paintings, stucco reliefs and mosaics which covered the walls, ceilings and floors of the houses. In particular, these interiors were dominated by their wall-paintings, which constitute, all in all, the most remarkable aspect of Pompeii and Herculaneum. They gave the houses in the towns, and the villas in the surrounding countryside, a specific and, to our eyes, a highly peculiar character. It did not seem peculiar to the Greeks and Romans, as would be clear enough if a greater number of their houses in other regions had survived. But it so happens that we have to depend very largely on Pompeii and Herculaneum for our knowledge of ancient interior decoration, because no Roman equivalents on anything like a comparable scale, and absolutely no Greek wall-paintings at all, have come down to us through the centuries. For painting, except in the less important medium of ceramics, is the most fragile of art forms, and the most unlikely to survive except in very special conditions. And so the deaths of the two cities, as Goethe remarked, were significant not so much for the transitoriness of life as for the perpetuity of art.

The average amount of skill displayed by the paintings is remarkably high, rising at times to magnificent. They seldom fail to be light, airy, gay and graceful, seeking to charm and succeeding in doing so, and suggesting a general, widespread high standard of visual civilization, which extended quite a way down the social scale, has never been exceeded in any subsequent age, and is very markedly superior

Painting on marble from Herculaneum in classical style, signed by Alexander of Athens. The goddess Latona (Leto) seems, against her will, to be accepting the hand which Niobe, assisted by Phoebe, offers her in an attempt to overcome her anger due to Niobe's claim to be her equal. Naples Museum

to what could be found in any town of comparable size today.

Indeed the only comparison that even begins to suggest itself is with Holland in the sixteenth and seventeenth centuries, when good paintings were likewise to be seen in fairly humble houses. But in Holland the pictures were separate easel-panels hung on the walls, whereas at Pompeii and Herculaneum they were painted directly onto the wall surfaces. The decoration of the house depended on them, and so did the plan of the architect – who himself played a large part in preparing their plaster bases.

For the first step in creating these pictures was to apply to the wall two or three carefully treated layers of limestone plaster, mixed with calcite and sand. Then the background of the picture was painted in, and left to dry. When it was dry, the figures and ornaments were added. The colours were mixed with soapy limestone, and some kind of glue and wax was added to create a shiny surface. By these means the paintings acquired great durability and brilliance. The pigments employed in antiquity were chiefly earth colours such as ochres, mineral colours such as carbonate of copper, and dyes of vegetable and animal origin.[1]

The technique was by no means an easy one to master, and required great alertness in the painter: he had to be able to put his ideas into effect rapidly on an extensive scale. The results appear impressive enough even today, but they must have looked a great deal better at the time. For we see the paintings at a disadvantage. Either they are in a museum – in most cases at Naples – or they remain in the rooms for which they were designed, at Pompeii and Herculaneum. But in a museum, however well lit and arranged, the impression is by no means the one the artist wanted to give, because these pictures were not intended to be seen in isolation from the rest of their wall and room; and if, on the other hand, they are left *in situ*, the ruined roofless nature of the houses means that the lighting is not what the painter had in mind – usually it is much too strong. The paintings were intended to be seen in a more subdued light; so that the required play of illumination and shadow can best be found, for example, in parts of the House of the Vettii, where the roofs have been restored. Here, then, the pictures can be seen more or less in the conditions for which they were planned, and the alluring effect of the colouring and the glaze can be fully appreciated.

However, the pictures were not original, in the modern sense of the term, or according to the Romantic nineteenth-century interpretation. They were adapted from the work of other artists elsewhere: the more important compositions were derived from Greek originals executed at some time or other during the preceding three centuries.

Painting had long been familiar in Campania and Lucania, where it can be seen on Greek or Samnite walls and tombs, as well as on vases.[2] A great deal of endeavour has been devoted to deciding whether and which of the paintings of Pompeii and Herculaneum should properly be regarded as Greek, Campanian or Roman. They should, in fact, be regarded as all three – with the proviso that some designs were known here in Campania before they ever got to Rome: though, conversely, the patronage provided by Roman rule later exerted a stimulating influence on Campanian artists.

The first sort of painting found at Pompeii, before 80 BC, was a plastic-looking imitation of variegated marble or alabaster or porphyry, executed in what is known as the Incrustation Style taking its name from *crusta*, a slab of marble. These sham inlays, predominantly red and black with a yellow lower strip, provide effective colour contrasts and a subtle play of abstract designs. At Pompeii, the style is found in the Basilica and the Temple of Jupiter, in addition to private dwellings such as the House of the Faun. At Herculaneum the same technique is cleverly employed in the Samnite House, blending well with the architectural proportion and harmony which these early mansions display.

The Incrustation Style recalls painted representations of coloured marbles in Greek houses built at the island-city of Delos during the late third and second centuries BC. Moreover, tombs of *c.* 300–280 in Egypt, near Alexandria, had revealed similar

Fig. 15. Map of the Ancient Mediterranean showing (in the eastern region) places of artistic importance to Pompeii and Herculaneum

MACEDONIA

Pella •
Palatitsa •

Olynthus

Samothrace

EPIRUS

THESSALY

Actium •

Pagasae •

EUBOEA

Thebes •

Aegina

Corinth •

Athens

Olympia •

ACHAIA

Delos

Thera

Aegean Sea

Troy •

Mt. Ida

ASIA

• Pergamum

• Myrina

• Smyrna

• Tralles

• Alabanda

Miletus

Cos

Byzantium

Euphrates

Issus •

SYRIA

Dura Europos

CRETE

JUDAEA

• Jerusalem

Alexandria

R. Nile

EGYPT

Below: This wall from the Villa of Publius Fannius Sinistor (or Lucius Herennius Florus) at Boscoreale displays dramatic masks which recall that this Second or Architectural style of painting seems to be derived from stage scenery. Naples Museum

Opposite: Harbour scene from Stabiae. Naples Museum. (See page 156)

Overleaf: The House of Lucius Ceius Secundus, Pompeii. Garden painted with an African landscape (see page 197)

designs, though these were painted direct on masonry instead of on a plaster-covered surface.[3] Originally no doubt this sort of imitation of marble, which became so frequent in Renaissance churches, was derived from the use of real marble facings in the lost Hellenistic palaces; and we learn that in the first century BC one of Caesar's commanders, Mamurra, decorated his house on the Caelian Hill at Rome with marble veneers of the same kind.

At Pompeii and Herculaneum the paintings in this style display tiny architectural features, such as the vertical division of the wall by pilasters. Subsequently, in one aspect of what is known as the Second Style – a phase which perhaps roughly covered the last three-quarters of the first century BC – this architectural theme takes over completely.[4] A wonderful series of pictures from a room in the Villa of Publius Fannius Sinistor, one of the numerous country mansions in the neighbourhood of Boscoreale (Chapter 5), represents the climax of the development. Now to be seen in the Metropolitan Museum of Art in New York, these pictures, each a masterpiece in itself, are divided off from one another by slim columns which give the whole room the appearance of a cloister court, looking out upon vivid, daring vistas of streets, houses, and columned halls.

There can be little doubt that these scenes are imitations of stage backcloths for dramatic performances, theatre sets of a type referred to by Vitruvius.[5] Comparisons from Campania can only be imagined: but it is relevant that Neapolis was an important centre of the drama. As regards Rome, the elder Pliny tells us of stage scenery which was probably by no means unlike these wall-paintings.[6] Set up by Appius Claudius Pulcher in 99 BC, it was said to include views of house roofs which were so realistic that even birds were taken in. The Greeks and Romans revelled in *trompe l'oeil*, and loved this sort of story. Backcloths of the kind reproduced by the Boscoreale painter remained fashionable in Roman theatres until elaborate pieces of actual architecture came to be introduced instead. Notable among these was the three-storeyed back-wall erected by the *aedile* Marcus Aemilius Scaurus in 58 BC. It was probably before this new fashion took effect, that is to say at some time during the first half of the first century BC, that the Boscoreale artist formed or borrowed the idea of giving permanent shape to the temporary painted stage sets.

However, architectural painting was not new in the Mediterranean world. Antecedents of this startlingly suggestive style are found in Egyptian tombs of the previous centuries, and another find in the same country, a schoolbook papyrus of Hellenistic times from Cairo, displays a painting of arcades.[7] But that does not mean that the style is specifically Egyptian, for it occurs in Delos and Judaea as well.

The Boscoreale paintings show a sort of spatial depth in which misty contours and diminishing colours are employed to indicate distance, and every building that is depicted in a picture shows its own parallel receding lines, based on separate vanishing points. This form of perspective is another feature of these works that can be traced back to Greek prototypes of the years following 300 BC. And they, in their turn, go back to theories and experiments which had come to a head in c. 400.[8] Until twentieth-century schools of painting revised doctrines of perspective, the Greek conceptions seemed a little hard to get used to, and indeed 'incorrect', because they had followed a different path from the accepted Renaissance 'correctness', aiming, in the way that has become so familiar to us, at the depiction of objects as they present themselves to the unifying human eye.

The twentieth century has again reached a hand backwards to the Boscoreale artist when it began to frame rooms in huge panes of glass which seek to abolish the wall. The ancient artists sought to do away with its solidity by another means: that it to say by painting the surface all over with wide prospects which seemed to give the little rooms a new spaciousness by opening a painted 'window' onto the outside world. It was fitting that these recessive scenes should be architectural, since it was as architectural spaces that artists saw the walls they were called upon to decorate. Their paintings, being mural, always have an architectural as well as a pictorial function. Even when they were not filled with actual pictures of buildings, as we have seen they sometimes were, this function was never altogether forgotten.

But the Boscoreale paintings provide not only architectural vistas but glimpses of rural scenes. At present, these landscapes are still minor features. But from now onwards they provide the commonest of all themes of Pompeian painting. The artists do not attain the excellence of scenes from the *Odyssey*, of the mid-first century BC, found in a house on the Esquiline

Masterpiece of landscape from Pompeii: *The Lost Ram*. Naples Museum

Hill at Rome. But the painter of those scenes had contemporaries at Pompeii and Herculaneum who showed a good deal of skill in opening up the wall with elaborate landscapes. What they most favoured was park scenery with hills and rustic shrines, and sacred trees in an enclosure, and herds and rustics dotted about – traditional idyllic themes spiced with an illusion of realism. This is very much the bucolic spirit of Virgil's *Eclogues*, written in the late 40s BC.[9] The elder Pliny refers to an artist named Ludius or Studius, or perhaps Spurius Tadius, whose achievement it may have been to bring pictures of this sort into fashion.[10] Like the architectural compositions, they gave added space to a room. The wide skies again bring the seventeenth-century Dutch painters to mind, though Renoir, when he saw these murals, had a different idea: 'It was Corot himself,' he declared, 'whom I found again intact in the Naples Museum!'

But often, too, the Pompeian landscapist came close up to his subject, and depicted the details of the gardens which his clients so greatly loved. Like the architectural painters, he seems to have been imitating theatrical scenery. The greatest surviving examples of this type of work, dating from between 40 and 25 BC, are the verdant, sylvan studies from the Villa of Livia at Primaporta, now in the National Museum at Rome.[11] But Pompeii, too, abounds in examples. They range from the tranquil paintings discovered in 1954 in the House of the Orchard, foreshadowing those French and Flemish tapestries known as *verdures*, to exotic and exuberant scenes of wild life. And, in particular, the gardens of these houses – in keeping with a principle that paintings should as far as possible reflect the purpose of the room or court to which they belonged – had their walls covered with pictures of flowers, shrubs and animals, which provided a sort of extension to the little gardens themselves, and made them look larger. This idea of painting nature is exploited with freshness and charm. But it was not new, for painted and sculptured garlands of fruit and flowers had been well-known at Pergamum as early as the second century BC, when the art of that kingdom of Asia Minor flourished so vigorously; and a Greek

painter called Demetrius, the son of Seleucus, who had been at Rome in 164 BC, was specifically called 'landscapist' *(topographos)*, the first man, we are led to believe, to bear this description. As a literary theme, landscape had already been made fashionable in the 270s and 260s BC by the idyllic poems of Theocritus of Syracuse, the pastoral poet of an urban civilization, writing for the townsmen of Cos and Alexandria and displaying a subtle blend of sophistication and simplicity, humorous realism and traditional convention – much the same blend as was later to emerge in the paintings of Pompeii and Herculaneum.

Amid the foliage of these pictures stalk birds. Herons are glimpsed between the pomegranates, and in the House of Fabius Amandio there is a group of three birds on the rim of a tall, marble bird-bath – one of many variations on a theme that was very familiar. Such paintings reproduced the real birds that these gardens often contained in their aviaries, and the artists who favoured these themes must have resembled one of the characters in Petronius' novel, a boy who was interested in two things: one was birds, and the other was painting.[12]

It was also fashionable to depict dead birds and animals and fish. They appear, with vegetables and fruit, in a remarkable series of still-life paintings – a subject (once again with Dutch analogies) which became, and then became again, a favourite theme of Pompeian painters. It was the custom to send gifts of uncooked foodstuffs, *xenia*, to one's friends,[13] and that is what these nature studies seem to represent.

Their treatment of the theme, skilfully combining realism and impressionism, probably owes something to a famous Greek painter of about the third century

Left: One of the garden paintings – often decorating the walls of real gardens – which became very popular from the later first century BC onwards. From the House of the Ephebe at Pompeii. Naples Museum
Right: Paintings of still life were among the most distinctive achievements of these artists. Birds and mushrooms from Herculaneum. Naples Museum

BC called Piraeicus, who had specialized in depicting commonplace objects – barbers' shops, cobblers' stalls, donkeys and food.[14] And at a slightly cruder level, the various shopsigns of Pompeii (Chapter 7) may likewise be indirectly indebted to his work.

But certain painters at Pompeii during the first century BC excelled in large compositions of human figures. Reference has already been made to the great religious paintings which covered three sides of a room in the Villa of the Mysteries (Chapter 4). Illustrating the mysteries of Bacchic initiation, they are based, to a large extent, on lost models from Pergamum. But the copyist, if that is what he must be called, was also a first-class artist, who had endowed his eerily remote figures with an extraordinary blend of divine dignity, violent motion, terror, magic, and exaltation.

It had been the achievement of the sculptor Praxiteles, in the fourth century BC, to give visual reality to the essence of an ideal world, creating figures which conveyed the otherness of the divine; and in the master-painter of the Villa of the Mysteries, working in the difficult medium of the mural, he had a worthy follower. The complex, arresting composition with which he covered these walls has rightly been called the greatest extant monument of ancient painting. Whether it dates from the time of Caesar (mid-first century BC) or from the earlier part of the reign of Augustus (BC 31–AD 14) has still not been determined.

Perhaps it was under Augustus that there developed a new and different Third Style of painting, which is likely to have overlapped chronologically with the Second and may have continued until about the time of Claudius (AD 41–54).[15] The artists practising this manner totally reversed the three-dimensional opening-up of space that had been favoured hitherto. Instead, they trace upon the walls a sparse, insubstantial, bamboo-like framework which echoes architecture only in a superficial, unfunctional and formalized sort of way; there is a considerable infusion of motifs – from Egypt, recalling Rome's conquest of that country in 30 BC – and its commercial and religious links with Pompeii (Chapter 4). For the time being, the architectural designs of earlier artists have become wholly subordinated to a flat, ornamental effect, recalling the tapestries and hangings which, as nails and hooks reveal, were employed to cover walls. These tapestries, a branch of the rich ancient art of textiles of which the almost complete loss represents one of the most serious gaps in our knowledge, sometimes had panels woven into their centres. And so the painters, too, who adopted this new style diversified their empty spaces by inserting small painted scenes at central points, such as the panels of landscapes and colonnaded villas on the walls of the House of Marcus Lucretius Fronto.

The landscapes of earlier wall-painters had sometimes been quite small, but now they are smaller still, and often have the miniature appearance of medallions; or, seen against their plain backgrounds, they almost look like the easel-pictures with which we are familiar today. Yet they were not easel-pictures, for they were still painted on the walls. That is to say, they still comprised a part, an integral part, of their backgrounds, however plain those were. To have hung framed pictures from cords and nails, as we do, would have seemed to the ancients an illogical and inorganic interference with the structure of the room. The nearest they got to this was to paint small pictures (*pinakes*) on especially fine stucco, for insertion at key-points in the general pattern of the murals. Such, for example, are the panels inlaid in the dining-room wall at the Villa of the Marine Gate at Pompeii. It was also possible to design special panel paintings for enclosure in frames, equipped with shutters which could open or close. But still these pictures were not hung; though they could be placed on a shelf or a ledge. Here is another artistic form found at the Villa of the Marine Gate, for one of its wall-paintings depicts a framed work of this kind executed in *trompe l'oeil* technique. Sometimes such paintings were done on marble; the Naples Museum possesses a particularly graceful rendering, in this medium, of girls playing a gambling game with knucklebones.[16] It is painted on two planes, and signed by one Alexander of Athens. Whether the signature means that he was the artist of this particular work, or of the original from which it was derived, cannot be determined; but the work is evidently a faithful copy of a painting dating back to the end of the fifth century BC – an unusually early model to choose. The shading of the women's clothes recalls Pliny's statement that this period, shortly before 400, witnessed the invention of shading by the Athenian artist Apollodorus. Another

Part of the painting on marble by Alexander. One of Niobe's daughters plays with knuckle-bones (*astragaloi*, four-faced dice), unaware that Latona is going to kill her and her sister and turn them into stone

Painting of Hercules and Telephus from the Basilica of
Herculaneum. Before a seated woman personifying
Arcadia, Hercules recognises an infant, suckled by a hind,
as Telephus, his son by Auge (a priestess of Athene)

Pompeian picture on marble, representing the slaying of the daughters of Niobe, displays a style which recalls some later model, painted at Pergamum towards the end of the third century BC.

When we come to what is described as the Fourth Style, this traditional designation becomes little more than a useless encumbrance. For it has to cover a whole host of different manners and types of paintings. Some of them started before the Third Style ended; and they were pursued simultaneously or successively from before the middle of the first century AD until the final destruction of the cities of Vesuvius. These were the styles in vogue before and after the earthquake of AD 62, and before and after the building of the Golden House of Nero at Rome (64–8), which

From *Hercules and Telephus:* the infant Telephus and the hind. The lively sensuous treatment contrasts sharply with the fierceness of the she-wolf which is often depicted suckling Romulus and Remus. Naples Museum

some of the paintings at Pompeii and Herculaneum foreshadow and others imitate. Since these Fourth-Style pictures belong to the last years of the towns, they have survived in larger quantity than examples of the earlier manners, and indeed the different varieties of Fourth-Style work, viewed as a whole, greatly outnumber all the others put together. According to one opinion, there were at least seventeen good artists all painting at one and the same time; and even if the number was somewhat less, a careful study of the pictures in one of the more important buildings, for example the House of the Dioscuri, shows a considerable variety of more or less simultaneous hands.

One characteristic of these artists is that they are reacting against the anti-architectural tendencies of the Third Style. That is to say, the new painters go back to the Second Style's architectural preferences exemplified by Boscoreale. But they only go part of the way back, because their own architecture is inclined to dissolve into fantasy. Sometimes, it is true, they produce realistic studies of buildings and towns, for example a charming sun-lit harbour view from Stabiae. But more often we see glittering sweeps of utterly unreal architectural inventiveness within filigree-thin lattice trellises: soaring, insubstantial structures of weird elaboration seen in airy perspective along precipitous vistas. Some of these designs – for example a glittering, fluttering composition from Herculaneum – are surely derived, like earlier paintings, from stage sets. One of the owners of the House of Menander, perhaps Quintus Poppaeus who was related to Nero's wife Poppaea, must have been a devotee of the theatre, for one of his rooms contains a picture of the dramatist Menander (who died in about 290 BC), identified by his name written on the hem of his robe and on the scroll he is holding in his hand.

Moreover, actual stage performances are now depicted on some of these walls. In the House of Pinarius Cerialis at Pompeii an entire surface is painted as a theatrical scene, on which a performance of Euripides' tragedy *Iphigenia in Tauris* is taking place against an architectural back-cloth. Though such themes, once again, go back to earlier Greek pictures, their popularity at this time may have been partly due to the passionate interest the emperor Nero took in acting and singing.[17]

The ancient myths were very far from dead. They still reached down to profound levels of conscious and unconscious feeling, and provided innumerable themes for a large range of artists at Pompeii and Herculaneum. These painters are imitating Greek originals, but they do so freely and imaginatively, with due regard for their own purposes and for the specific environments in which they were working. Their exercise of this freedom is proved when we are given a chance, as we sometimes are, to compare two or more Pompeian copies, taken from one and the same original: sometimes the copies differ markedly from one another.[18]

The Greek models employed by the Pompeian painters, known to them from art collections, repertoires and pattern books, are not usually derived from the great masters of the classical fifth century BC, but tend to be drawn from their successors of subsequent epochs. Some of these Greek artists had lived and worked in the fourth century BC, including the time of Alexander the Great (who died in 323). Others belonged to the third and second centuries, and often included exponents of the court art at Pergamum, which, as we have seen, prompted a painting of the daughters of Niobe, and above all inspired the mighty Dionysiac composition at the Villa of the Mysteries. Because of these borrowings, it is to Pompeii and Herculaneum that we are indebted for almost everything that we know about the schools of Greek art which successively flourished during the last four hundred years before the Christian era.

The artists who copied and modified these earlier works at the two Vesuvian towns mostly remained unidentifiable. It is very rare for them to sign their names. A certain Lucius records that he painted *Pyramus and Thisbe*[19] and other pictures in the House of Loreius Tiburtinus; but he is not one of the best. A far more gifted artist, who shares the general anonymity, was the painter of *Hercules and Telephus* from the Basilica at Herculaneum. Boldly drawn and painted, adroitly shaded and high-lighted, this elaborate yet satisfying composition is entitled to rank as one of the masterpieces that have come down to us from antiquity. In Hercules' recognition of his infant son Telephus, borne to him by Auge, a priestess of Athene, there is no lack of feeling; and the suckling of the baby by a hind is movingly rendered. But the emotion or sentiment is expressed with classical restraint, and through the medium of a clear, three-dimensional, classical technique.

Other paintings create their effects by less straightforward means. A picture of Perseus and Andromeda, for example, though its forms are again solid and statuesque, is bathed in a soft luminosity which hints

Perseus and Andromeda – a classical yet also romantic
composition from the House of the Dioscuri at
Pompeii, copied from a work of the fourth century BC
by the Athenian Nicias. Naples Museum

158

The animated style, from the House of the Vettii: Pentheus torn to pieces
by the worshippers of Dionysus for his disbelief. Naples Museum

at a different approach, suggesting an atmosphere that is romantic rather than heroic. Other works are far more openly emotional and indeed sensational. The *Death of Pentheus*, torn apart by Maenads, clearly lent itself to this treatment. And so did some of the more dramatic scenes of the Trojan War. This Homeric saga, the foundation of all Greek and Roman education, was particularly dear to Nero,[20] who, in addition to his alleged adoptive descent from the royal house of Troy, himself wrote a poem on the theme of the *Iliad;* and he is said to have declaimed another as he gazed upon the Great Fire of Rome in AD 64. *The Sacrifice of Iphigenia*, from the House of the Tragic Poet, is full of histrionic drama and distress. *Achilles Surrendering Briseis* suggests tension and psychological suspense.[21] *Ulysses and Penelope* shows the disguised wanderer displaying almost uncontrollable perturbation at the sight of his mother. And one of the greatest pictures that has survived from the ancient world is a boldly coloured painting from the House of Menander, which, displaying a powerful economy of detail, tells the story of how the Trojan Horse was insinuated into the doomed city. This was also a

subject for the poets of the day; and Petronius, poet as well as novelist, is one of those who handles it:

> Then, lo, Apollo spoke and Ida's wooded flanks
> Were felled, the forest seaward dragged, and the tall trees
> Chopped and shaped to make a horse of war, a giant bulk
> Within whose mass a cavelike hole was hollowed out.[22]

The Pompeian painting is full of the spirit of this Neronian age. It is redolent of Seneca's sense of suffering and sadness and undeserved fate; and it breathes the dramatic eeriness and mystery of his nephew Lucan's epic poem *The Civil War (Pharsalia)*. The Wooden Horse itself is sinister and gaunt. A shrouded moon gives out a ghostly, foreboding gleam, and a flickering light comes from the torches of the long-robed women in the centre. Otherwise the whole landscape is dim and dark, and so are the towers and walls that loom up above the scene. But from the shadows emerge two strong lines of dramatic movement. The urgently leaning figures in the

The Trojan Horse, from Pompeii. In the middle of this hauntingly dramatic, impressionistic composition are seen four Trojans pulling the wooden horse, in which Greek warriors are concealed, into their doomed city. Naples Museum

foreground contrast sharply with the static figures in the penumbra beyond.

In such pictures the volumes are broadly blocked out, faces and emotions are impressionistically suggested by a few bold strokes of the brush, and myth is infused with a new and vivid life. These successes are originally owed, no doubt, to the Greek forerunners of these painters, and particularly to the Pergamenes and others who had first gone in for such spectacular exploitation of chiaroscuro and human feeling. The painters of Pompeii and Herculaneum are imitating these artists; but in doing so they are evidently improvising as well, with a skill that almost deserves to be regarded as original achievement.

Some of the personalities in these mythological paintings are very vigorously and subtly expressed. *Hercules and Telephus*, for example, displays a remarkable interpretation of Hercules, looking at his little son with an air of fairly sympathetic surprise. And the youthful figure in the same picture, playing his pipes behind the blank-faced seated figure of Arcadia, is the satyr to end all satyrs: an excellent, if rather sinister, example of early imperial Italy's passion for portraying children. (Painted medallions showing the features of small boys and girls have been found in numerous parts of Pompeii, though many are now crumbled away and lost.)

In pictures with non-mythological subjects, too, there are powerful delineations of character. An outstanding example is a philosopher, in a painting from the sumptuous Villa of Publius Fannius Sinistor at Boscoreale (*c.* 40 BC). He stands aloof watching a discussion beween two figures, who appear to be personifications of Macedonia and Persia. The original had been painted two or three centuries earlier for one of the dynasties that followed Alexander, presumably the Antigonids of Macedonia, in which case the philosopher may be a certain Menedemus of Eretria (*c.* 319–265 BC). But the Boscoreale artist has infused into his study a rare, untheatrical sort of dramatic feeling, an intense and vibrant immobility, which must be to some extent his own.

Left: Detail of *Hercules and Telephus* from Herculaneum. Arcadia, whose head appears here (in the company of the notable young Satyr), is intended to glorify the city of Pergamum in Asia Minor, which traced its origins back to the Arcadian Telephus. This picture at Herculaneum was based on a Pergamene painting

Philosopher from the Villa of Publius Fannius Sinistor at Boscoreale. Independent and austere, he is gazing at two figures (in another part of the picture; they have been interpreted as Macedonia and Persia). Naples Museum

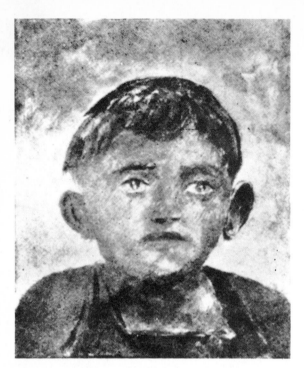

Above: A sad small boy, example of a keen interest
in the portraiture of children, from a wall in Pompeii;
the picture has now disappeared

Right: The Roman sentimentality towards children is again
displayed in this relief of a sleeping boy from a
fountain in the Via di Mercurio. Pompeii Museum

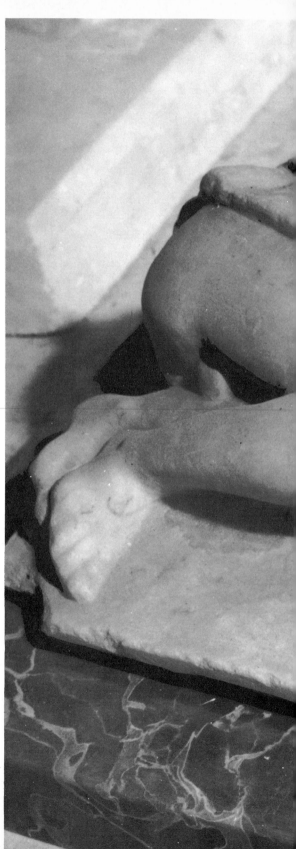

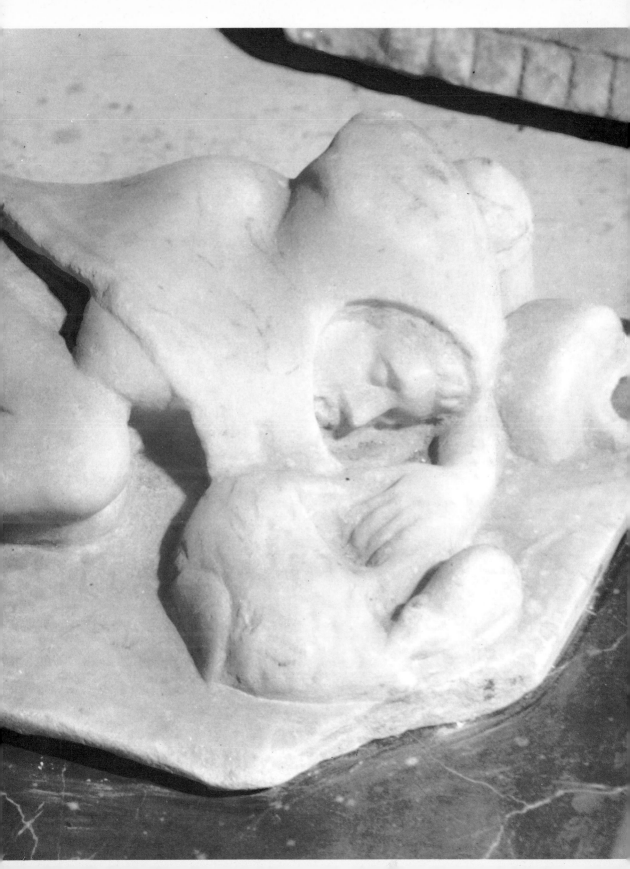

The head of a young girl with book and pen, painted in about the middle of the first century AD, has again caught a meditative mood with sympathy and skill. But here the artist is more interested in brushwork than in psychology or physical realism. Very different is the double portrait of the lawyer Terentius Neo and his wife, convincing masterpieces of the realistic tradition of portraiture which was, and remained, such an outstanding achievement of Roman Italy. The young couple seem to bring ancient and modern Mediterranean humanity very close together; and here at least there is no question of dependence on any earlier Greek original.

Painters in villas outside Stabiae, as recent excavations have shown, belonged to an independent tradition which reacted away from the more straight-

Opposite: Portrait of a married couple from Pompeii; the lawyer Terentius Neo and his wife. Naples Museum
Below: Girl with tablet and pen from Pompeii (wrongly described as *Sappho*). Naples Museum

Above left and right: The artist of these portraits from the Villa of the Obsidian Vases (S. Marco) outside Stabiae displays a highly distinctive, emotional style, with clever use of shading. The head on the right may represent Theseus. Antiquarium, Castellamare di Stabia
Opposite: Small Cupids or *putti* are characteristic of later Pompeian taste. House of the Vettii

forward and realistic schools in much the same way as the impressionistic mythological scenes were modifying the more classical interpretations of mythology. These villas have disclosed a whole series of intensely conceived heads of remarkable power displaying stronger colours, more vigorous facial expressions, and more emphatic and emotional exploitation of light and shade than can be found in portraits from the other places. Features are only sketched and suggested, with the eyes profound pools of colour, mirroring unknown depths of the spirit.

Yet the art of this region was not entirely, or even principally, a serious art. It is true that a painter of the time was working for clients who were remarkably alive to the higher points of harmony and good taste, especially in aesthetic matters. But what these patrons really wanted was just to enjoy the walls of their houses; and they were able to appreciate a sophisticated and mildly malicious light-heartedness. Since this was the attitude for which an artist had to cater the details he inserted are often the best part of his picture. The most attractive figures are not always the full-sized statuesque representations, but the tiny beings who perch or balance on the steeply curving

balustrades and architraves that frame the surfaces of the walls. This is a witty, ironical, undemanding art, attaching particular importance to delicate rapidity of touch.

The paintings executed during the last decades of the life of Pompeii, Herculaneum and Stabiae show an amazing diversity of bold, fluent, and skilfully graded colours. In considering the art of this epoch it may ultimately, when much further study has been undertaken, become possible to detect a certain evolution of fashion. For example, it is already evident that in the last years of all a strong taste for black and white effects was developing. In the House of Loreius Tiburtinus, one of the latest works presents a series of medallions of the Seasons, mysteriously suspended on an evanescent architecture against large white panels. New ideas of illumination were also being tried out, and artists decorating the House of the Vettii make buildings look as if they stood in a ravine flooded by light, amid vast profound perspectives. Infusing a fresh animation into the traditional pastoral landscapes of shrines and trees, the new impressionistic ideas produce masterpieces like *The Lost Ram*. In this picture the two figures, man and ram, appear like

shadows in front of the light walls of the sanctuary, against a romantic landscape of wild gorges and caverns.

At a less ambitious level there was much decorative work pure and simple – paralleled in the superb stucco low-reliefs which are another feature of private houses, in addition to their extensive appearances at public baths. An earlier penchant for Egyptian themes was also revived and developed, revealing a special taste for more or less fantastic landscapes of that country. No doubt this fashion existed elsewhere as well; but Pompeii, with its Egyptian connections, was likely to be particularly receptive.[23] Flooded Nile waters are to be seen, and sycamores and palms, pygmy figures and wild beasts. Animal paintings in general, exotic and otherwise, were very popular, especially in gardens; the Houses of Marcus Lucretius Fronto and Lucius Ceius Secundus display a whole fantastic Africa. Moreover, as a visit to the room devoted to the subject at the Vatican Museum readily shows, the ancient Italians excelled not only at painting animals but at sculpting them as well; a goat from the Villa of the Papyri, and a neat sprinting bronze pig, and horses' heads from Herculaneum, are all fine examples of this

An example of the graceful stucco work
which blended with paintings and mosaics to form
the decoration of Pompeian houses (see page 175)

Opposite : The artists of the early empire show deep sympathy with animals. The head of one of the bronze horses which were harnessed to a chariot upon the pediment of the Basilica at Herculaneum. Naples Museum
Below : One of four ornaments (goat, lion, snake, deer) on a fountain at Nuceria Alfaterna (Nocera). Naples Museum

art. Moreover, as in the hunting circles of later epochs, love of animals was curiously combined with a taste for seeing them brutally killed. The House of the Stags at Herculaneum bears that name today because of two sculptural groups of stags attacked by hounds. They are skilful, tense pieces of work, but not everyone will agree with the expert who has described them as admirable examples of decorative taste.

The walls at Pompeii and Herculaneum, then, had no easel pictures, because they were painted with murals instead. It is true that the walls were also sometimes adorned with textiles. On the floors, however, there were few textile coverings; in other words they did not go in for carpets. The Italians knew of eastern carpets, through intermediaries such as the Alexandrians, but the appearance of the floors in the Campanian towns shows that they made little use of them.[24] For, instead, it was evidently the intention of the architects to cover the floors with a decoration as integral and structural as the paintings which adorned the walls. The medium employed was the mosaic, which became one of the most characteristic and successful arts of the Roman world.

Quite a large number of Greek mosaics of the late fifth and fourth and early third centuries BC have been discovered in Greece (Olympia) and Egypt (Alexandria), but particularly at Olynthus and other centres in Macedonia (Palatitsa, Pella). The subjects are mythological scenes, or animals, or floral designs. They are not yet worked, like later mosaics, in cut cubes, but use is made of black, white or polychrome natural pebbles. Mosaics made of small, equal-sized cubes of coloured stones and marbles (opus tessellatum), arranged in straight lines in their beds of cement, became gradually known to the Greek world during the decades following the conquests of Alexander. Probably the idea came from the east, although Sicilian origin has also been suggested. The predominant conception was reminiscent of textiles – though now the idea was transferred to a more permanent medium. That is to say the mosaic, or its pictorial part, was thought of as a sort of rug let into the middle of the floor-space, this central panel being known as the emblema. Or it could be like a mat beside the door.

In Italy, however – we cannot tell if it originated there or not – people began to form a different interpretation of what such mosaics ought to be like. The floor was now envisaged as a unified space, to be covered all over by a mosaic, which thus resembled a

Opposite: The House of the Mosaic Atrium, Herculaneum. The black and white pavement and central basin or impluvium (beneath the roof opening) were forced out of shape by the weight of the volcanic mud
Below: Fig. 16. The House of the Mosaic Atrium, Herculaneum

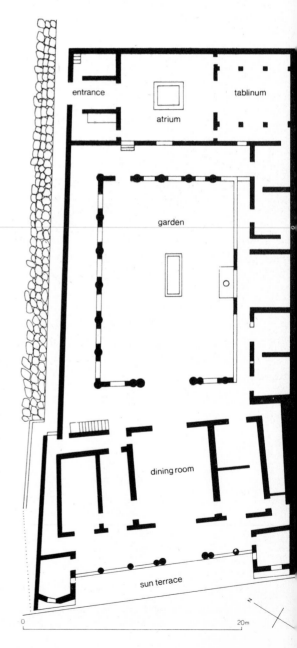

entrance

atrium

tablinum

garden

dining room

sun terrace

0   20m

arpet rather than a rug or mat. This formula is
articularly found in the *atria* of the large Samnite
ouses built at Pompeii and Herculaneum in the
econd century BC, though the structure of these
uildings required, in a sense, a compromise between
he two types of mosaic, because the basin in the
entre is a sort of substitute for the rug-like central
anel. Thus in the *atrium* of the House of the Faun at
ompeii, when it was first rebuilt after 200 BC,
xcavation has now revealed (1961–2) that there was
 pavement of tile fragments and mortar mixed with
ood ash, into which simple geometrical designs

formed by pebbles were inserted *(opus signinum)*.[25] In
the *atrium* of the Samnite House at Herculaneum the
basin is surrounded by a floor of similar material. But
then came the House of the Mosaic Atrium, which
displays a true 'tessellate' mosaic with a geometric
pattern of black and white checks (later on, there were
sumptuous geometrical arrangements of marbles, as
in the House of the Relief of Telephus). This sort of
overall pattern was the form of mosaic that tended to
prevail in subsequent centuries, and specimens from
all over the Roman world represent its various manifestations.

Variegated marble floor in the House of the Relief of
Telephus, Herculaneum

But the cities of Vesuvius are also able to provide a
number of extremely remarkable examples of the
older Greek 'rug' technique: that is to say, of mosaics
– inserted in the centre of the floor – which form
pictures and not merely decorative patterns.

Sometimes these pictures could be very large. The
most famous of all, showing the Battle of Issus (333
BC) between Alexander the Great and the Persian
monarch Darius III, measures 3·20 × 5·50 metres.
Dating from about 150 BC, this mosaic was found in the
House of the Faun at Pompeii, and is now in the
Naples Museum. Together with the later and more
purely decorative Nile mosaic at Palestrina (the
ancient Praeneste), this is the finest example of the art
that has come down to us, and reveals the impressive
potentialities of the medium – even if it seems slightly
uncomfortable that one should have to look down
onto the floor to see such a complex design. This

battle-piece was adapted, perhaps quite closely, from
a Greek picture which was painted soon after the
battle of Issus, or at least before the end of the fourth
century BC. Possibly the artist was a certain Philoxenus
of Eretria.[26] In any case, this mosaic gives us a better
idea of what a major Greek wall-painting must have
looked like than we can obtain from anywhere else.

Philoxenus was known for his 'short-cuts', illustrated by the half-hidden figures in the mosaic. The
composition is elaborate but brilliantly lucid and
dramatic, with bold foreshortenings and effective
highlights. Large mosaic pictures of this kind were
presumably executed on the spot, by imported Greek
experts – unless, perhaps, Neapolis occasionally had
a man or two of its own who was capable of rising to
such heights. The grand sweep of the composition has
inspired comparison with a scene painted by
Velasquez, *The Surrender of Breda*. But the airy baroque

Floor mosaic from Pompeii illustrating the fashion for Egyptian scenes – like the famous
Nile mosaic at Praeneste (Palestrina). Late first century BC. Naples Museum

Floor-mosaic of the Battle of the Issus (BC 333) between Alexander the Great and Darius III of Persia;
adapted from a painting of the fourth century BC; from the House of the Faun, Pompeii. Naples Museum

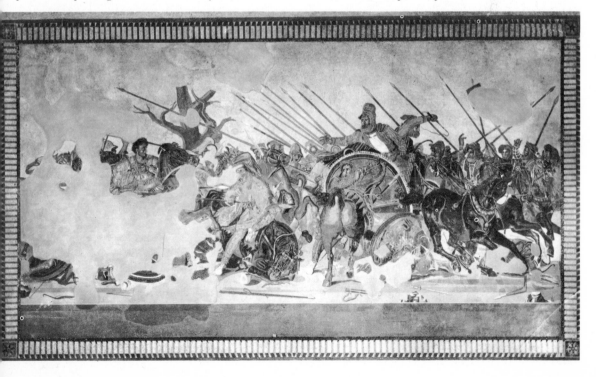

Detail of the Alexander mosaic

perspective of the seventeenth-century work is lacking in the ancient mosaic, in which there seems to be nothing but foreground

In important works such as the Alexander mosaic the cubes do not always proceed in straight lines, but vary in direction, as in size, to suit the artist's requirements. Other, much smaller, panels, carry these variations a good deal further, and achieve an additional, almost painter-like, delicacy by their employment of cubes of

a wide range of shapes (usually rounded) and an equal variety of dimensions (often very small), arranged in series of sinuous curves. Two little mosaics employing this 'worm-like' technique *(opus vermiculatum)* were found in a country house outside Pompeii misleadingly known as the Villa of Cicero, and are now in the Museum at Naples. They are signed by a certain Dioscurides of Samos, though it is not clear whether he was the maker of the mosaic or the painter of the original Greek picture from which it was copied,

One of a group of masked actors preparing for a play. Naples Museum

which, to judge from the style of the imitations, might be dateable to *c.* 280 BC. One of these two works displays a group of street musicians, accompanied by a wan, sickly-faced child. The other shows an old masked sorceress handing out advice or a love-potion to two girls; the whole party have tightly clenched hands. Overlapping strips of black, grey and yellow represent an attempt to show spatial depth.

These panels are mounted on marble trays and were therefore prefabricated. This presumably means that they were imported ready-made, perhaps from the Greek east. The designers of such works must often have had pattern-books in front of them, but what these were and how they were used we cannot tell. Another panel shows pigeons perching on a cup, a well-known theme already encountered in paintings. It had been initiated, we are told, by a certain Sosus of Pergamum, who was also famous for a painting of an unswept dining-room floor that is reproduced in a number of mosaics.[27] One example, in the Vatican,

Signed by Dioscurides:
mosaic of a sorceress and her client

bears the signature of a certain Heraclitus. In this case, the man who signed his name was evidently not the original painter, who was Sosus, but the designer of the mosaic.

Even if the scattered fragments of food on the floor are rather too significant of the dining habits of the day to be altogether savoury, they perhaps stand for a better aesthetic idea than the major figure compositions of what a floor design ought to be like. And even more satisfactory, from this decorative point of view, are the scenes of marine life intended for houses and baths. An excellent example of this genre shows a fight between an octopus and a lobster, while a moray *(murena)* watches for the moment to attack, and other fish swirl all round.

Yet one of the most remarkable of the small Pompeian floor-mosaics uncompromisingly recoils from this conception of the mosaic as an ornamental pattern. Originally located in the centre of a bedroom floor, it displays the portrait of a female, described by

Mosaic of an underwater scene. In the centre, a fight between an octopus and a lobster. Naples Museum

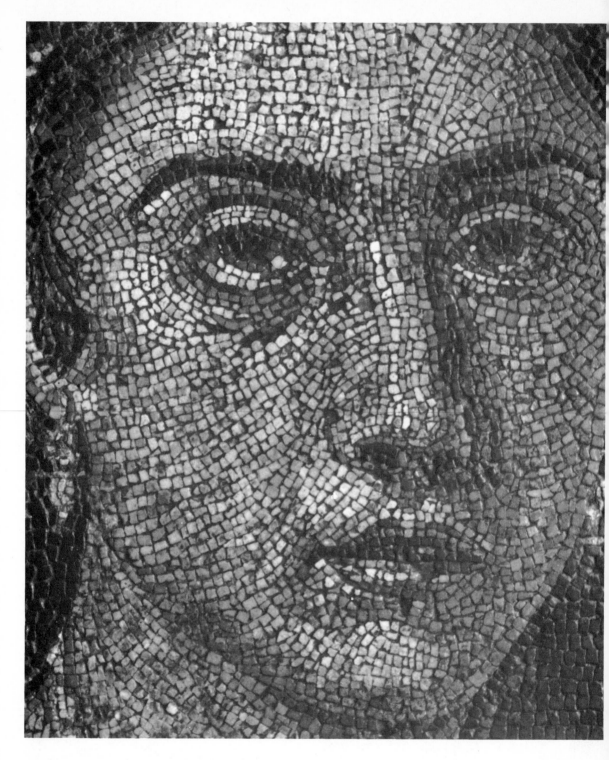

Above and opposite: Unique floor-mosaic from Pompeii
depicting a skilful portrait of a woman. Naples Museum
Overleaf: A brothel at Pompeii. Inside there are
pornographic paintings and graffiti

Anthony Thorne as 'a harassed-looking disk-eyed woman, by no means beautiful, who appeared to be about to say something important in a low voice'. The head bears a considerable resemblance to the earliest of the great series of painted mummy-portraits from the Fayum and elsewhere in Egypt, which, as far as we know, were just beginning their long history at the time when Pompeii and Herculaneum ended theirs.[28] But earlier Egyptian examples, unknown to us, may have influenced this Pompeian portrait, just as so many other influences from Egypt came into Campania. Indeed, for all we know, the mosaic (or the design on which it was based) may itself have been brought to Pompeii from Egypt ready-made; or, alternatively, this type of portrait originated neither in Egypt nor in Campania, but in some other regional school of art of which at present we have no knowledge. The work is rich in nuances and luminosity.

In the early Byzantine empire, four and five centuries after the destruction of the Vesuvian towns, one of the world's major art forms was to develop from the idea of transferring mosaics from floors to vaults and walls. But the transference had already begun in Pompeii and Herculaneum – and no doubt elsewhere also at the same time, but it is on these two places, as so often, that we have to rely for almost our entire knowledge of what was happening in the Graeco-Roman world. These wall mosaics are particularly to be seen in and around the niches adorning fountains in the courtyards of the private houses. The mosaics are worked in cubes of glass paste and marble, often varied by framed lines of seashells. The designs tend to be geometric, with small figure scenes introduced at certain points. Such compositions, for example those in the Houses of the Large Fountain and Small Fountain at Pompeii, must have produced dazzling effects in the summer sun. The House of the Neptune Mosaic at Herculaneum boasts a particularly elaborate three-niched grotto or *nymphaeum* faced entirely with colourful mosaics, including hunting scenes; the figures are designed against a mainly blue ground. In the same courtyard, at right angles to the grotto, is a more ambitious essay in the same medium, a large-scale wall-panel showing Neptune and his wife Salacia (Amphitrite). It is executed with naturalistic modelling and shading to create the illusion of a painting, and the outer part of the mosaic consists of a gorgeously ornamental, polychrome framework, which contrasts amusingly with the academic ordinariness of the figures.

Above: Mosaics were used for vaults and niches as well as floors: the House of the Large Fountain, Pompeii
Opposite: The summer dining-room of the House of the Neptune Mosaic at Herculaneum. Neptune and Salacia (Amphitrite) appear on the right. The niches at the end, forming a grotto dedicated to the nymphs, are faced with mosaics of deer chased by hounds

Wall-paintings and mosaics not only did the service that easel-paintings and carpets perform today, but their incorporation in the general design of a building was based on the assumption that furniture would be relatively sparse. And so it was; even the richest house would have seemed bare by most modern standards. Larger quantities of furniture, and larger pieces, would have distracted attention from the effects created by the architects and artists. And in any case there was little room for such a thing – even the couches and table for the diners must have made dining-rooms uncomfortably full. The equivalents of modern wardrobes and wall-cupboards, therefore, were generally provided by niches, alcoves, and small adjoining rooms.

However, such furniture as there was showed an extremely good quality of design, without any sign of our modern distinction between 'good' and mass-produced pieces. The standard forms of earlier Greek furniture were only slightly changed by the Etruscans and Romans, but the Italian products were superior to the Greek in finish and workmanship. There were more beds or couches than there are nowadays – for sleeping, dining, studying and resting – and the dining couches in particular were often the most precious articles in the house. Frequently they were inlaid in rare woods, and fitted with gold and silver intaglios. Their bronze mountings and legs, curved more often than rectangular, are well known to us from Pompeii and Herculaneum, and so, in carbonized form, are

Day-couch in the House of Menander, Pompeii

their wooden frames – though these give an inadequate impression of the original elegance of the couches.

Beds for sleeping in were higher than ours, needing steps or a stool, but dining couches were quite low. They were a Greek institution first introduced into Italy by Cnaeus Manlius Vulso after his expedition to Asia Minor in 189–188 BC. Easterners had been inclined to say that the Greeks did not know how to make a comfortable bed, and when we see the remains of the couches of Pompeii and Herculaneum comfort is not the first thought that comes to mind. But the day-divans, which sometimes had raised sides and backs, were well upholstered with mattresses and cushions; and beds were protected by wooden panels at the head and one side, to keep off the damp of the wall. They were also softened by fine-combed wool mattresses placed on ropes slung in wooden slats. And the second-century scholar Pollux of Naucratis suggests to us how much we have missed owing to the disappearance of every ancient bedspread or counterpane. He calls them delicate, well-woven, glistening, beautifully coloured, covered with many flowers, covered with ornaments, purple, dark green, scarlet, violet, rich with scarlet blooms, purple bordered, shot with gold, embroidered with figures of animals, gleaming with stars.[29]

Most of the other furniture in the houses was made wholly of bronze.[30] Its high standard of execution might have been expected from the proximity of Capua, which was the great manufacturing centre for such objects and supplied them far and wide, even beyond the frontiers of the empire. Pompeii also brought bronze furniture from Neapolis, in addition to manufacturing its own on the spot. One round table seems to have been acquired from Rome, since it is inscribed 'made for Publius Casca Longus' – one of Julius Caesar's assassins. When, after the collapse of the Republican cause at Philippi, Casca killed himself, his property was no doubt put up for auction by the winning side; and this table may have been bought by a citizen of Pompeii at the sale. It is easy to see why the Pompeian tripods and tripod tables, with their combination of crisp lines and ornate decoration, attracted imitators in the years following 1800.[31] Goethe, when he visited Pompeii, had particularly admired the 'high, slender bronze pedestals, evidently intended as lampstands', with feet shaped into claws or hooves, and sometimes adjustable sliding upper parts. There were also richly ornamented bronze braziers and heating apparatuses.

Three legged table in the *tablinum* of the House of Paquius Proculus, Pompeii

Silver cup with designs of olive-twigs (from the treasure found in the Villa La Pisanella at Boscoreale) showing a love of naturalistic designs shared by contemporary painters. Louvre

188

Head of Apollo on a silver mirror, part of the treasure found in the House of Menander, Pompeii

The silverware, too, was both grand and exceedingly abundant in some of these houses. At least five silver treasures have been found in the area during the past century and a half. In 1895 a country mansion at Boscoreale, La Pisanella, yielded not only over 1000 coins but 108 embossed silver vessels, contained in half-buried urns.[32] These silver objects were bought by Baron Edouard de Rothschild, and subsequently most of them found their way to the Louvre. They comprise many pieces of fame and distinction, including, for example, the cups decorated with skeletons (Chapter 4), and a bowl framing a sculptural portrait (Chapter 8), and pieces with designs referring to the glory of the imperial house.

Then, in 1930, a further treasure of 118 silver objects, again with a hoard of coins, was discovered in the House of the Menander at Pompeii. Among them were seven especially fine pairs of drinking vessels, adorned with figure scenes in relief. The discovery was made after a ten-year-old boy had crept into a hitherto unknown underground room of the house; and there the treasure was found, arranged in sets inside a nail-studded chest, with nearly every item carefully wrapped in coarse canvas. An analysis of the whole collection shows a wide range of different periods and artists and places of manufacture. Some of the cups and bases may be of local origin, made at Neapolis or at Pompeii itself. Others come from much farther afield, and in some cases from the east where Hellenistic silver work of this kind had flourished in Alexandria and the coastal centres of Asia Minor.

These great finds at Pompeii illustrate the mania of Italian collectors for Greek metalware and their willingness to pay extravagant prices, based on the weight which was frequently indicated on each vessel. In 189 BC Lucius Cornelius Scipio, celebrating his Triumph over Antiochus III, King of Syria, was accompanied by henchmen carrying ornamental silver plate weighing 635 kilos; and thereafter the influx of silver into Italy steadily continued. Goldwork, remarked Pliny, brought nobody fame, but the metal that mattered was silver, on which many famous artists were accustomed to lavish their attentions. The reliefs are often masterly, and not always too solemn; cups engraved with olive twigs from Boscoreale, and others from the House of Menander displaying pastoral scenes, achieve the same light touch as paintings of similar subjects.

As regards decorative wares other than silver, the most outstanding example to have survived is a vase

The Blue Vase, made of cameo-glass; found in a tomb outside the Herculaneum Gate of Pompeii.
The designs show Cupids harvesting the grapes

of white-on-blue cameo-glass found at Pompeii in a tomb outside the Herculaneum Gate. Like later paintings in the House of the Vettii, it shows a mimicking of adults by Cupids, the baroque *putti* whom the Roman love of children whimsically elevated into an artistic form. Here they are seen at the wine-harvest; some are plucking the bunches of grapes, while others tread the juice of the vats. How important this activity was to Pompeii will be suggested in the next chapter.

'Come to the Sign of the Bowls' (*Ad Cucumas*). A wine shop in the main street of Herculaneum. Some of the wines are listed, with vintage dates

7. Farms and Trades

The imposing country-houses dotted round Pompeii and Herculaneum and extending along the Bays of Naples and Salerno – *villae urbanae*, in which the owners did not live all the year round – often had agricultural quarters as attachments (Chapter 5). A further category of rural estate centred upon buildings which were farms rather than mansions, but had luxurious, or at least comfortable, apartments within the farm-houses to provide for occasional visits by the owner, in addition to the less elegant permanent accommodation for his agent, who was a freedman or a slave. A third type of property, about which we have a detailed literary record from Varro, was the real farm-house, designed for a farmer-owner who lived there all the year round.

Our knowledge of these farms hardly goes back beyond the last years of the Republic, and we cannot trace very many of them. But such a place, of the more substantial sort, has been identified at Boscoreale. The court or farmyard of this *Villa Rustica* was surrounded on three sides by porticoes. On its left are dining-room, bedrooms (probably occupied by slaves, since the best bedrooms are likely to have been upstairs), and an elaborate bathing establishment, in which the arrangements for heating the water have been completely preserved. Beyond were stable and kitchen (which was often, in these farmhouses, the principal room). Straight ahead of the courtyard stood the wine-presses. To the right of the yard was an open court for fermenting wine (frequently there was a second court, for watering animals) and beyond lay bedrooms, oil-press and olive-crusher. Away to the right was a barn and a threshing-floor. Apart from this open space the total area of the farm was about 23·50 by 45·50 metres.[1]

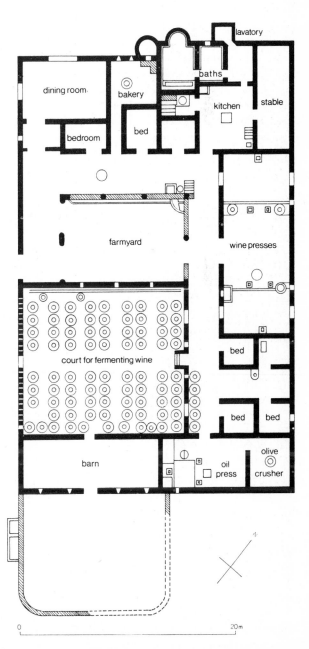

Right: Fig. 17. Farm (*Villa Rustica*) at Boscoreale

At the neighbouring Villa of Agrippa Postumus at Boscotrecase, a slave-barracks for agricultural workers has come to light, containing eighteen small rooms (the number must have been a good deal larger elsewhere) and a prison-cell with stocks, which were fortunately not in use at the time when Vesuvius visited destruction upon the place.[2] The eruption wiped out all the country mansions and farms of the area, and similar invasions have taken place from time to time in later centuries; for example in 1906 two lava streams destroyed a hundred houses. At Reginna Minor (Minori), across the Lattari mountains on the Bay of Salerno, rustic villas excavated during the years 1950–4 were subsequently reburied by a flood, but then partly uncovered once again.[3]

But another so-called villa, outside the Vesuvian Gate of Pompeii, seems not to have been a villa at all but a whole group of separate agricultural dwellings. Indeed, the entire région adjoining the town was filled with farms and little villages or rural suburbs; in three cases their names have been identified.[4] And indeed, even inside the city-walls, the latest excavations have revealed a large vineyard, in the quarter known as the Foro Boario north of the amphitheatre. (Round the ancient roots there are holes, like those which Italian farmers still dig in the ground in order to retain the water.) But this wine-growing within the gates must have been unusual. Outside the town, on the other hand, the fertile lower slopes and surroundings of Vesuvius were dotted thickly with medium-sized or small agricultural concerns. They produced wine, olives and cereals, as well as a brand of tall, thin-stalked cabbage for which Pompeii was famous; and hemp, almonds and various kinds of fruit were grown as well. An ancient farm at the little agricultural centre at Gragnano, just behind Stabiae, made cheese as well as wine, and has yielded the best and most scientific grain mill which has so far been discovered.[5]

Shops in the Via dell'Abbondanza, Pompeii

Unquestionably agriculture was the most important feature of Vesuvian life. There is no good reason to suppose that the Campanian soil had become exhausted by the first century AD. Nor is it probable, as has also been suggested, that the comparatively large scale of capitalist activity had involved any appreciable increase in landlord absenteeism.

Inside Pompeii itself, in the most ancient days, commerce had probably been more or less concentrated within the district round the Forum. Then, at least as early as the second century BC, the trading area was enlarged in a north-west direction. Little shops, looking out onto the street, were inserted into the façade and flanks of the noble House of Sallust; and this practice became customary elsewhere in the town. Tenants were either strangers, or the householder's own dependents (*clientes*), or his slaves. The Stabian Baths in the same town let out a similar row

of shops. It was only a question of time before the main street, the Via dell'Abbondanza, became transformed from a row of dignified domestic façades into an almost unbroken series of shops and taverns, with slender partitions, external shutters, upper floors, and projecting balconies. But the best surviving illustration of this development is provided by the House of the Neptune Mosaic at Herculaneum, where the collapse of the front wall revealed an entire shop with all its contents. Moreover, owners let out their premises not only as shops, but also as inns and baths. A notice at the entrance of the Villa of Julia Felix at Pompeii describes the baths that the proprietress offered for hire as 'good enough for Venus'.[6]

This was a town where trade served as a leveller, and many prosperous families were heavily engaged in such pursuits. Above all, they were busy selling their agricultural produce. Many of the large townhouses depended closely on a country background

Shop for wine and cereals attached to the House of the Neptune Mosaic at Herculaneum

Shops opposite the House of the Vettii, Pompeii

The sign of a wine-shop, or wine-merchants' corporation, near the Forum of Pompeii

and backing. The Vettii, for example, owners of a number of different kinds of concern, produced various brands of wine from their numerous farms; and the decoration of their mansion inside Pompeii, with its jocular designs of Cupids harvesting, shows how little they were ashamed of this activity. It is true that the Vettii were new-rich,[7] but inscriptions on wine jars show that some of the most prominent old Samnite families at Pompeii were just as deeply concerned with the wine-trade.

The vintages from various parts of Campania rank supreme in the elder Pliny's lists of Italian wines, and among them the products of Vesuvius occupied a good place.[8] Many jars label their contents 'Vesuvium' or 'Vesvinum', the forerunner of the Lacrima Christi which now comes from these slopes – though surprise has been expressed that such an agreeable wine should bear the sad name of 'the Tear of Christ'. On the way up the mountain, warned *Baedeker's Guide*, this Lacrima Christi 'is offered for sale at nearly every cottage, but had better not be partaken of before the ascent'. In ancient times there was a kind of grape-vine which was particularly associated with Pompeii and produced wine known as 'Pompeiana'.[9] This was a large-scale product enjoying a considerable reputation, though Pliny gave it a maximum of ten years' life and declared that it gave one a headache which lasted until noon the next day.[10] No doubt, as always, quality varied; inside a drinking-shop in the ancient town an un-

satisfied visitor scrawled up on the wall. 'Inn-keeper of the devil, die drowned in your own piss-wine!'

At Boscoreale there was a large country inn, producing its own wine (and its own graffiti as well),[11] and within the towns the wine-shops and taverns were very numerous. At Pompeii twenty have been identified, and 118 bars – far more than in Ostia, for example, where people tended to drink in their corporation-houses or clubs instead.

The taverns in Pompeii, which, like the shops, were often rooms rented out from a large private house, did not themselves store wine on an extensive scale. Instead, they drew upon the big cellars of the farms outside the walls, one of which, at Boscoreale, possessed a capacity of over 100,000 litres. At the Villa of the Mysteries the jars were protected by woven straw, like modern Chianti flasks (in places where plastic has not appeared instead). In the taverns of the town, the wine likely to be needed in the near future was kept in large clay jugs which had pointed ends so they could be kept cool in circular cavities underneath the polychrome marble counter. Furthermore, many of these wineshops, including the Inn of Asellina, which is the best preserved, were equipped to serve hot wine, to which the ancients were addicted; at Asellina's a kettle for heating it up was found with the lid still hermetically closed.

In this establishment, when Vesuvius erupted, the bronze petty cash was left behind in a drawer. We do

Men playing dice on an inn-sign from Pompeii. 'I've won', says the man on the left. 'It's not a three, it's a two', says the other. (In the next picture the inn-keeper is seen pushing them out of the door). Naples Museum

not know if the barmaids got away to safety, but we do know what they were called – Smyrna, Maria and Aegle. And not only have their names survived on the walls, but so have sums showing customers' debts.

'Suavis demands full wine-jars, please,' remarks a graffito on the wall of a wineshop, 'and his thirst is enormous.' In addition to their front bars, these taverns might also have dining-rooms at the back, and gardens where the clients could sit and watch cabarets of girls who danced and played the castanets and pipes. In front, as at the entrances of English inns, there were painted sign-boards. 'Come to the sign of the Bowls,' proclaims a Herculaneum wineshop, and Bacchus is shown on the sign with a half a dozen samples of various types of wine. Their prices are often specified on these notices, the famous Falernian brand from north-western Campania being the most expensive.[12] A resort near the Nucerian Gate bears the sign of a gladiator.

The Inn of Salvius offers its visitors a rather forthright hint, by displaying pictures of customers gambling, quarrelling, and eventually ejected from the premises. For in spite of restrictive laws, which were evidently obsolete, gambling played an extremely active part in the day-to-day life of Pompeian inns; and it was also very prominent in the public baths. There was even an association of dice players.

'At Nuceria,' reads a graffito, 'I won 855 sesterces at dice – no cheating.' In a gaming house in the Via Stabiana we can see the names of two women and the amount they owed, including the rate of interest and a note of the dates at which they incurred these debts.

The farm which had room for over 100,000 litres of wine also possessed enough storage jars to keep 5,910 litres of the local olive-oil. During the second century, BC, when the elder Cato was writing about farming, Campania had become an important region of olive culture, and this was a more important industry in the region round Pompeii than it is at the present day. The local lava made particularly good olive crushers,[13] and most of the farms near Pompeii and Stabiae had their own presses and vats. The product came into town, and was no doubt used at the numerous cook-shops which provided cooked food and snacks to take away or eat on the spot, like the modern *tavola calda*.

Some of these places were deplored by ancient writers for their squalor, but in view of the inadequacy of domestic cooking facilities they were a great convenience. Oil was also sold in the shops, and so were fruit and vegetables, of which a substantial store, comprising beans and chick-peas, has been found inside large round jars in the shop attached to the House of the Neptune Mosaic at Herculaneum (see page 193).

Left: Part of a picture of a dinner-party. Naples Museum
Right: An olive-crusher of Vesuvian lava, designed to separate the pulp of the olive from the stones. The two wheels, linked by a wooden cross-piece, rotate round an iron pin fastened in a hollow lava basin. Outside Pompeii Museum

Mill and bakery, Pompeii. The mill consists of a conical lower stone which served as an axle and an upper, biconical stone which was turned by two handles. The oven is on the left. Pompeii Museum

Another large container in the same establishment is still full of its ancient cereal. Bread had come into general use during the second century BC (it also served the purposes of a spoon, in addition to its employment for the fumigation of stuffy rooms). The bread people now began to eat was made of a more refined wheat than the unhusked emmer which had given early Italians their porridge. Barley, too, was employed; and there were at least ten different kinds of bread, and a brand of dog-biscuit as well.

In the bakery of Modestus at Pompeii eighty-one circular rolls of bread, each patterned in eight segments, were found intact in a sealed and almost airtight oven; they can be seen today in the Naples Museum. The private baking-ovens of old mansions were gradually replaced by smallish or medium-sized independent bakeries *(pistrina)*, of which forty have been discovered at Pompeii, some installed in what had formerly been private houses. They normally included heavy stones for grinding the grain, a room for kneading dough, an oven for baking,[14] and a shop for selling the finished product. Vesuvius was as famous for its millstones as for its olive crushers. They consisted of a hollow stone placed on top of a second stone which was fastened in a masonry base. The grain was poured into the upper stone, which could be rotated, so that the grain was ground fine between the two stones and came out at the bottom as flour. The rotation was effected by two horizontal arms which were attached to the upper stone and which were turned, on occasion, by animal power. But very often there was no room for a donkey, and then slaves had to do the job. 'Work, work!' scrawls one of them, 'and you had better, too!' But it was a painful and detested task. Moreover, bakeries and their neighbourhoods stank very unpleasantly, because the bran was thrown out into the street just outside, to be eaten by pigs.

A very important industry at Pompeii was wool. The Monti Lattari (Lactarii), which close the southern end of the Bay of Naples, take their name of 'milky mountains' from the numerous cows they pastured; but there was also much grazing of sheep, and the Campanians inherited from the Samnites an interest in manufacturing woollen clothes. Brought into town, the wool was taken to one of the numerous factories which had been set up, like the bakeries, in what had previously been large houses. The material was washed and stretched and thickened and dyed,[15] and cleaning operations were undertaken as well. These various activities of 'fulling', one of the most widespread ancient crafts, were sometimes all carried out simultaneously in one and the same place, or sometimes they were distributed among separate establishments.

This whole process of the drapery trade was painted on the walls of a mill belonging to Lucius Veranius Hypsaeus, who dried his fabrics on brick pillars between the Corinthian columns of a spacious *atrium*. A colleague, Caecilius, rented his premises from the town of Pompeii, and entrusted them to his freedmen. Another man in the same line of business, Stephanus, used his upper floor and courtyard for drying; in the walls are holes for the canes over which the wet clothes were hung, and near the entrance stood a pressing board worked by a pair of large wooden screws. Built in at the back were small vats for treading the dirty clothes, and larger vats for rinsing. The clothes were treated with carbonate of soda, potash, fuller's earth, and human urine, which male passers-by were encouraged to supply through jars hung on the wall.[16] Across the way from Stephanus was a painted shop-front of the cloth merchant Marcus Vecilius Verecundus. His shop sign, beneath a representation of Venus Pompeiana in a chariot drawn by four elephants, shows various scenes relating to his industry, including a picture of his wife in conversation with a female customer. Verecundus (or a neighbour) was also a felt-maker, whose products in this material were in demand for caps, cloaks, slippers, blankets and horse-blankets. Use was made of vinegar or some other fixative, which was first heated by a stove and then worked into the wool by men standing

The decoration of the doorway on the Building of Eumachia, centre of the fullers' guild beside the Forum of Pompeii

naked to the waist in shallow troughs. Thus impregnated and matted together, the stuff was then pressed and manipulated until it acquired the necessary consistency of texture.

Right in the middle of the town, looking out over the Forum, the fullers had their own corporation centre, the richly adorned three-apsed Building of Eumachia, standing in a large court surrounded by a two-storeyed colonnade. The central apse contained a statue of Livia, the widow of Augustus, in the guise of Imperial Concord (Concordia Augusta), a personification to which, in association with Piety, the building was dedicated by Eumachia and her son. It was a wool market, anticipating the corporation halls of later Venice, its *scuole* and *fondachi*. Outside the Nucerian Gate, Eumachia had a splendid tomb. It was found sealed, but her ashes were not inside it; what happened to them and her we do not know. But at all events, as far as our knowledge goes, she seems to have played a more important part in the history of Pompeii than any other woman. The gold and jewels the local ladies wore were splendid and elegant, and they formed electoral pressure groups (Chapter 8), but female public personages were evidently rare.

The remaining local trades possessed another fine centre just up the Forum, the provision market or *macellum*. This was a large porticoed space containing shops, chapels, auction-rooms, a meeting place for the priests of Augustus' cult (Chapter 4), a money changers' booth, and displays of fruit and vegetables. The models for this type of centre were the *macella* at Rome, one named after Livia and the other built by Nero and depicted by him on a coin. In the middle of the Pompeian building was a small, twelve-sided, domed building with a water-tank, connected with the sewers. Inside the tank, fish-scales have been found. Here, then, was the fish-market.

Like Herculaneum, where many nets and hooks have come to light, Pompeii devoted a great deal of attention to fishing. A painting found in a recently excavated household shrine depicts the boats on the Sarnus – which was at that time a navigable stream, and received worship as a divinity in many Pompeian homes. The painting also shows porters carrying products to be loaded upon the vessels. The principal fishing harbour must have lain near the mouth of the river, which was then some one and a bit kilometres from the Stabian Gate. Remains of warehouses and of buildings adorned with painted walls and lined with wine-jars have also been found at a secondary harbour along the coast, where skeletons wearing gold ornaments testify to unsuccessful attempts to get away during the eruption.

The ancient Italians preferred fish, if it was good enough, to every other food; and the speciality of the

Coin of Nero, showing his new Provision Market (*macellum*) at Rome – a grander version of the *macellum* in Pompeii

Pompeians was a concentrated fish sauce, which appealed to the ancient taste for sharp flavours. The sauce was made as follows. The entrails of sprats or sardines – the parts that could not be used for salting – were mixed with finely chopped portions of fish and with roe and eggs, and then pounded, crushed and stirred. The mixture was left in the sun or in a warm room and beaten into a homogeneous pulp until it fermented. When this *liquamen*, as it was called, had been much reduced over a period of six weeks by evaporation, it was placed in a basket with a perforated bottom through which the residue filtered slowly down into a receptacle. This end product, decanted into jars, was the famous *garum;* the dregs

left over, also regarded as edible, were known as *allec*.[18] But there was a great variety of different fish sauces. At Pompeii, a certain Zosimus sold containers for the whole lot of them. But the principal merchant in this field, as the inscriptions on many jars show, was Marcus Umbricius Scaurus, a public benefactor and provider of gladiatorial games whose tomb outside the Herculaneum Gate was erected by the town council.

'Papilus' breath,' writes the poet Martial, 'is so strong that it can change the strongest perfume into *garum*.'[19] In view of this unfragrant aspect of local industry, it is a relief to add that a further speciality of Pompeii,

Shop-sign at Pompeii: a procession of carpenters

as of other centres along the bay, was scent. Roses and other flowers abounded in the gardens of the town, and in the surrounding countryside they supplied a large flower and perfume industry.[20] This was one of the activities of the Vettii, in which the Cupids painted in their dining-room are seen to be engaged.

Other recorded guilds include fruiterers, garlic-growers, wheelwrights, woodmen, carpenters, and plumbers (who must have been highly skilled). There were also taxi-men, whose conveyances had a stand outside the gates. And many of the narrow streets, as well as the square beside the amphitheatre, were crammed with peddlers and hawkers operating from makeshift stands.

Pompeii, then, was a very active place. It had been active ever since its gradual industrialization during the second and first centuries BC. The writers of graffiti frankly scrawl a mercantile philosophy on the walls, embodied in the slogans: 'Gain is Joy!' and 'Welcome Gain!'

Like neighbouring towns, the place had its market day, every eight days; a list giving the time-table throughout the whole area has been found written up in a shop. Naturally relations between the various townships of the region were close. Thus the Pompeians depended on the furniture industry of Capua and perhaps Neapolis. They also drew upon the terracotta factories of the island of Pithecussae

Writing materials on a painting from Pompeii. Naples Museum

(Aenaria, Ischia), and depended on the glass-manufacture for which the Campanian river Vulturnus provided beds of suitable sand.

However, Pompeii was able to look further afield as well, particularly because it had the advantage of lying outside the customs limits of Neapolis and Puteoli: a fact which, as various Egyptian elements have suggested (Chapters 4, 6), did not prevent its population from taking a special interest in the shipping from Alexandria which came to the latter city. Lamps were purchased from north Italy, and a large amount of pottery from Gaul,[21] while recent discoveries have revealed that during the second century BC there were pots of Spanish provenance as well. Nor were the Pompeians satisfied with the oil and wine that they themselves produced. For, in addition (herein resembling the people of Stabiae) they obtained oil from southern Spain,[22] and they imported wine as well, including the products of Spain, Sicily and Crete. An ivory statuette of Lakshmi, an Indian goddess of good luck, has also been found in the town. It belongs to a category of objects associated with the Kushana capital of Mathura, south of Delhi, and must have come from some Indian port such as Barygaza (Broach, near Baroda).

Early in its history, Pompeii had served Greek traders as a trans-shipment point for Campanian exports, and no doubt it performed a similar service for the Etruscans. But its own exports did not usually get very far. However, the odd jar of Pompeian fish-sauce, or piece of Pompeian furniture, appears in Rome; and locally found coins of Massalia (Marseilles) dating from the fourth century BC, as well as pieces issued on the Balearic island of Ebusus (Ibiza) about fifty years before our era, had perhaps been given in payment for products of Pompeii purchased in those foreign ports.[23]

For the visitors who brought this money, or their commercial wares, to the town there were remarkably numerous hotels – far more than could be found at any place of the same sort of size today. The largest hotel so far identified, on a winding street near the Forum, had room for fifty guests (though they sometimes had to sleep up to four in a room). The ground floor portions of such establishments were often disposed round two sides of a courtyard, with a kitchen on the third side, while the bar and restaurant were in separate buildings a short distance away. Two large hotels, just inside the Herculaneum and Stabian Gates, each had their own dining-rooms, bedrooms,

stable, water-trough and garage-shed for waggons. In the building by the Stabian Gate the upper rooms could be reached discreetly by a side-entrance, an advantage for those who wished to introduce women, a practice which, to judge from graffiti, was scarcely discouraged by the management. In a disreputable quarter of Pompeii one of the principal hotel-keepers was a certain Sittius, member of an old Campanian family from Nuceria which had provided Julius Caesar with a shady freelance general.

Although Pompeii was a busy place, its economy was never very massive. When the eruption occurred and people got away with what they could, the largest number of gold coins found in anyone's possession was no more than sixty-nine, carried by a man who succumbed near the Small Theatre or Odeon. Money treasures in the houses, too, are not enormously large; a find of fifty-five gold and 987 silver coins is exceptional. And the sums mentioned in business documents are likewise fairly modest. The most valuable evidence in the latter field is provided by about 150 wax tablets discovered in a broken-down chest in the House of Lucius Caecilius Jucundus, the rich banker-auctioneer whose splendidly vulgar portrait is still to be seen at Naples Museum – unless the bust represents his father Lucius Caecilius Felix, who founded the family fortunes as freedman-agent of the aristocratic Caecilii. The tablets, mostly bound in threes and sealed, are carbonized, but the imprint on the wax, which had been pressed into the wooden frame and thoroughly smoothed, penetrated into the wood, and there is hardly a document in the whole collection that has not proved decipherable. For the most part they consist of receipts for loans or rent-payments relating to lands, pastures and manufacturing concerns.[24]

The banker Lucius Caecilius Jucundus (or his father); bronze head found in his house at Pompeii. Naples Museum

8. Public Life and Sexual Life

Right up to the last moments of Pompeii the local political life of the town was intense. In Rome, from the dictatorship of Caesar onwards, there had usually been little or no real competition for the annual elected office of consul, because, behind the scenes or even overtly, the choice was made by the ruler. Herculaneum, too, does not seem to have had much political activity. But the situation at Pompeii was remarkably different. The holders of its two pairs of top jobs, the *duoviri* and *aediles*, took office on 1 July every year, after elections had been held in the preceding March. Already in the late Republic Cicero had remarked that it was harder to get into the Pompeii city council than into the senate of Rome itself, and in the imperial epoch rivalry for the chief municipal posts remained extremely keen. Probably this was true of most of the self-governing communities of the western empire until their autonomy withered away in the second century AD. But here at Pompeii the vigour of the struggles may have been accentuated by a Samnite tradition of vociferous democracy. The Samnites had often been loudly critical of their officials, and a speaker in Petronius' novel tells how the tradition was kept up in the Campanian town where Trimalchio was supposed to have lived – which was probably Puteoli. 'No one,' says this man, 'gives

Opposite: Column of Phrygian marble erected by a pair of *duoviri* (leading officials of the town) in the precinct of the Temple of Apollo. Old sketches show a sun-dial on the top; Apollo was the Sun-god
Left: A leading local citizen mocked: graffito from the Villa of the Mysteries

a damn about the way we're hit by the grain situation. To hell with the aediles! They're in with the bakers – you be nice to me and I'll be nice to you. So the little man suffers . . . This place is going down like a calf's tail!'[1] That is very much the discontented spirit in which someone has written up on a Pompeian wall:

Here's my advice. Share out the common chest.
For in our coffers piles of money rest.[2]

At Pompeii the *duoviri* could, on occasion, get into worse trouble than popular criticism. In AD 59, the disturbances in the amphitheatre (Chapter 3) compelled them to resign.[3] This was bad luck, but at least they had not paid for the show. Often enough, that was what the chief officials of towns had to do, for the sponsorship of gladiatorial games was the best way to win and keep popularity. Moreover, one Pompeian official is on record as having given the civic treasury a large sum after his election was successfully completed; and a painting shows another functionary personally conducting a free distribution of loaves at a bakery.

But the first problem was how to get elected. About this process we know a very great deal, because the walls of Pompeii are plastered with election propaganda. Nearly three thousand electoral inscriptions have survived. More than half of them relate to the very last year of the town's existence, AD 79, because after each successive annual election such appeals had normally been obliterated to leave room for the next batch. The notices were painted, in capitals, in red or black paint on a white plaster ground, or in white upon red. They were executed by professional notice painters, who were also responsible for official announcements in the Forum. These notices covered matters such as lost property, slave auctions, police regulations, sentences of criminals; there is a mural which shows a placard of this kind stretching across three equestrian statues in a row. One such artist, Aemilius Celer, has painted his name on the wall of his own home; there are also inscriptions cursing men who smudge public announcements.

The voters in the annual elections seem to have included all adult male citizens, voting as individuals or in corporations. While the candidates themselves remained coyly silent (in contrast to modern elections), every one of their dependents or 'clients', the men who used to sit on the benches outside their houses

Opposite: An official of Pompeii seeking popularity by making a free distribution of loaves. Naples Museum
Below: Election propaganda and announcements of gladiatorial shows on the walls of a street leading to the amphitheatre at Pompeii

and call on them each morning, had to be active in their patrons' favour. Moreover, all the major trades and industries associated themselves with electoral appeals; and so did the priests of Isis, porters, muleteers, bath-stokers and even the beggars.

Marcus Calatorius: a leader of the tiny town of Hercula-neum depicted like a noble Roman. Naples Museum

Women, too, though they lacked a vote themselves and rarely reached the eminence of the powerful Eumachia (Chapter 7), are well to the fore with electoral slogans. These female canvassers included the girls who worked in Asellina's restaurant; and even prostitutes added their word. Some of the manifestos are very strange. 'Claudius' little girl-friend,' we are told, 'is working for his election as duovir'. And 'Vote for Lucius Popidius Sabinus,' declares another poster, 'his grandmother worked hard for his last election and is pleased with the results.' Were these inscriptions put up by the opposition trying to make fun of Claudius and Popidius?[4] The same suspicion crosses one's mind again when the walls of an inn, next door to the Forum Baths, declare that a certain Vatia is recommended by 'the sneak thieves', the 'whole company of late drinkers', and 'everyone who is fast asleep'. These may, however, have been the authentic, if whimsical, names of smart social clubs, to which people of leisure belonged. Even children were mobilized by their teachers to join in the campaigns: 'Teacher Sema with his boys recommends Julius Simplex for the job. Sometimes we are told that a prominent man is lending his support to a candidate; on other occasions he is urged to do so. 'Proculus, make Sabinus aedile, and he will do the same for you.'

A number of portrait busts give an idea of the sort of men who got elected. Like the painted portraits of Pompeii, they are well up to the magnificent standard reached by Greek, Italian and eastern artists during the first centuries BC and AD. Philodemus, the Levantine philosopher who lived in the region (Chapter 4), wrote treatises on psychological characteristics,[5] and the bust of Lucius Caecilius Jucundus or his father (Chapter 7) might well be an illustration of such a treatise. The rocky physiognomies of two Herculanean notables, Lucius Mammius Maximus (who presented the town with its covered market) and Marcus Calatorius, shocked the great eighteenth-century archaeologist Winckelmann because he found them so far removed from the standards he regarded as classical.[6] These dignitaries are certainly made to look pretty grim, like senators in the capital. In fact, however, the great men of Pompeii and Herculaneum, whether they belonged to the old nobility or to the mercantile class which was gradually superseding them all the time, probably carried little or no weight in Rome – or even in Neapolis or Puteoli. It is true that Lucilius Junior, the Pompeian to whom Seneca wrote his *Moral Letters*, became an important civil

This portrait probably depicts an ancestor of the Augustan owner of this silver plate. Part of the Boscoreale treasure in the Louvre

servant. But it was a quite exceptional piece of good fortune when a woman connected with the Pompeian house of the Poppaei produced a daughter, Poppaea, who got herself married to Nero.

She was evidently popular in the town; and so was Nero himself, who loved this coast and particularly Neapolis. 'Good luck to the decisions of Nero . . . of the emperor and the empress!'; 'Primogenes remembers Nero Caesar in his prayers'; 'Campylus wishes all good health to Poppaea'[7] – though there had also been a good word for Octavia, who was murdered to make room for her: 'Please God be kind to Octavia the emperor's wife.' But an undercurrent of irreverence is also to be seen. At the Boscotrecase Villa of Agrippa Postumus, someone has inscribed a wall with the somewhat perilous remark: 'The mother of Caesar Augustus was a human being.' And the ruling house, which claimed to be descended from Trojan Aeneas, might not have liked a painting at Stabiae showing that hero, and his father and son, with the heads of dogs or apes. Worst of all, a silver cup said to have come from Pompeii shows pairs of male figures who unmistakably display the facial features of the imperial family, engaged in making love with one another.[8]

It is a characteristic of graffiti, all over the world, that they go in a lot for sex; and this applies with overwhelming force to the inscriptions scratched with stilus, iron nail, wooden splinter or toothpick upon the walls of Pompeii. Some of the citizens of the place thought there was too much of this sort of thing, though a number of such objectors had recourse to further graffiti themselves in order to make their point.

I wonder, wall, that you do not go smash,
Who have to bear the weight of all this trash.[9]

A certain Septumius employs the same medium to launch obscene attacks upon anyone who reads his scrawl, and even upon passers-by. And many householders understandably felt a strong aversion to this form of self-expression, inscribing their houses with the direst warnings against everyone who wrote on their walls.

However, such protests were of no avail, and graffiti abounded. They covered a wide range of human activities. But, in particular, they dealt with every possible aspect of emotional and sexual life. It is touching to learn, from the walls of a hotel, that Vibius Restitutus slept there alone, and longed for his

Urbana. But one wonders if he is to be identified with the man of the same name who, we read elsewhere, 'has many times deceived many girls.' Staphylus, again, places himself on record in two different places; he had a rendezvous with a woman called Romula at one, and with a certain Quieta at the other. Virgula tells Tertius that she finds him repulsively ugly. Livia (surely not the venerable widow of Augustus) asks Alexander if he really thinks she would mind in the slightest if he dropped down dead tomorrow. Sometimes there is a note of romance: 'Noete, light of my life, goodbye, goodbye, for ever goodbye.' Less romantic is a woman who writes: 'Fortunatus, you sweet little darling, you great fornicator, this is written by someone who knows you!' At the entrance to the front lavatory at the House of Loreius Tiburtinus someone has been inspired to proclaim: 'May I always and everywhere be as potent with women as I was here!' Expressions of sexual preference are also frequent. At least six inscriptions compare brunettes with blondes. Others put forward a wide assortment of opinions on the same general theme.

I like a girl with a proper mat, not depilated and
    shorn.
Then you can snuggle in well from the cold, as
    an overcoat she's worn.[10]

The Baths have their own abundant store of graffiti. Xanthe is told that the masseur knows all about how to tickle, and Colepius, who kept the Forum Baths at Pompeii, is accused of taking deplorable liberties with women. The back room of the Suburban Baths at Herculaneum contains an enigmatic record: 'Apelles the waiter dined most pleasantly with Dexter the slave of the emperor, and they had a screw at the same time.' Or does it mean 'together'? the philologists are undecided. Homosexual inscriptions are very far from uncommon; yet the former, heterosexual, interpretation may be true, because it is a peculiarity of Pompeian obscene paintings (of which there are many in a closed room at the Naples Museum) that a third party is often present during copulation. This is a practice which, although specifically disapproved of by Herculaneum's resident philosopher-poet, Philodemus, recalls the voyeurism clearly detectable in Petronius' novel about this part of the world. The theme occurs not only in paintings but in numerous graffiti. Often they are rather better executed than their modern counterparts, though the graffitists of today cannot always do themselves artistic justice owing to the technical difficulties presented (intentionally) by the tiled or rough-cast walls, and varnished doors, of modern public lavatories.

All the numerous Latin equivalents of four-letter words are found over and over again; in certain cases the indexes of graffiti that have been painstakingly drawn up note the recurrence of some such term as often as sixty or seventy times. The Oscans, who had once lived in this part of the world, enjoyed a special reputation for obscenity. But perhaps the same thing would have been found in all ancient towns, if their graffiti had survived on a Pompeian scale.

On the ramp leading to the House of the Relief of Telephus at Herculaneum appear the words: 'Portumnus loves Amphianda. Januarius loves Veneria. We pray Venus that you should hold us in mind. This only we ask you.' At Pompeii, too, a thread that runs strongly through the graffiti, which is perhaps not so noticeable on similar inscriptions today, is the vigorous and often indignant stress the writers lay upon their right to love and be loved. It could not be for nothing that Venus was the protectress of the town (Chapter 4).

One aspect of her patronage was very extensive prostitution, a state of affairs explicitly disapproved of by only a few pagan writers of antiquity. A brothel at Pompeii (which women, nowadays, are not usually allowed to visit) is full of obscene paintings and graffiti; the latter variously expressing aspiration, boasting and disappointment.[11] Malcolm Lowry, in the *Present Estate of Pompeii* (1949), complained that these brothels were by no means spacious, and 'seemed to have been made to accommodate the consummations of some race of voluptuous dwarfs'. Notices written up at many points of the town, including the vestibule in the House of the Vettii, indicate the rates charged by prostitutes, which were mostly very cheap. [12] Hotels, bars and baths likewise catered for the same demand. And there is likewise much talk of prostitution in the novel of Petronius.

He also has a great deal to say about another local phenomenon, the phallus. The basic plot of Petronius' *Satyricon* revolved round the god of gardens, Priapus, generally represented with a huge erection. Parodying Homer's 'Wrath of Poseidon against Odysseus', Petronius supposes that his own impotent anti-hero is suffering from the wrath of Priapus, and the phallic theme recurs continually in the book. And at Pompeii,

too, phalluses were to be seen all over the place. Erect penises, painted and sculpted, stood in every part of the town (many of them have now been removed to Naples). These representations, measuring all possible lengths from four feet downwards, appeared on the sign-boards of brothels, taverns and shops, on dyers' vats, above the doors of houses, on the statues

A phallus, emblem of good luck, protruding from the wall above a Pompeian door

Tripod with legs in the form of sexually excited satyrs, from a house at Pompeii. Such erections were ubiquitous in domestic art adorning fountains, on lamps and bell-pulls and sauceboats, on the satyrs who form the legs of bronze tripods, and of course on graffiti as well. 'Handle with care' is the label inscribed on one such picture scrawled up in a snack-bar.

To describe all these phalluses as merely obscene is not enough. Seen by every ancient inhabitant every day of his life, they reflect an attitude which did not find sex mysterious and felt few inhibitions about the subject. They were also symbols of the fertility of nature, suitable for barren women to wear as amulets. And above all they were safeguards against the evil eye (disguised as ox-horns, they still appear in the same capacity today – hidden in handbags, or attached to key-chains, or hung round the necks of children and horses). But understandably, when all these emblems at the Vesuvian towns first came to light, they contributed to a widespread belief, in eighteenth- and especially nineteenth-century Europe, that these places had been exceptionally wicked. They fortified the opinion voiced by the famous headmaster Dr Thomas Arnold, in 1840, that the Bay of Naples was a 'fearsome drama of Pleasure, Sin and Death'; and his son Matthew Arnold, too, believed that the life of the two places was so unremittingly sensuous and sensual that it would, in the end, have 'fatigued and revolted us'. This one-sided view of Pompeii and Herculaneum as the scenes of more or less incessant orgy has appealed to innumerable writers of novels and films.

With further reference to graffiti, it must be added that large numbers of them show a high degree of literacy not to be found among their counterparts today. The fact that even some of the least exalted sentiments are dressed in a kind of verse is not itself indicative of lofty culture.

> Chius, I hope your piles are chafed once more,
> That they may burn worse than they've burnt
>   before.[13]

But sometimes the verses are more poetical and romantic; a graceful piece of nostalgia was quoted in Chapter 4. Poetry especially flourished on the walls of Pompeii's Basilica, recalling Martial's observation that the spaces on walls are the only hope for a poor unpublished poet.[14] But another significant feature is the frequency of quotation from the great poets. Tibullus and Ovid appear, and part of a line of Virgil – 'All were silent' – is cut off in the middle of a word: was the writer overtaken by the eruption? Greek, too, occurs: in the largest shop at Herculaneum there is a quotation from Diogenes. Today this would be strange; modern graffitists show little taste for Wittgenstein or T.S. Eliot.

By measuring the position of the graffiti on the walls, one can detect that some of these excerpts from the classics (though only a relatively small proportion) were scratched up by children, eager to show off their knowledge. Other children wrote rude remarks about their teachers; and at the House of the Silver Wedding in Pompeii, there is a warning that if you don't like Cicero corporal punishment will inevitably result.

Childrens' drawings on a wall of the Villa of the Obsidian Vases (S. Marco) at Stabiae

Epilogue

It was a long time before any part of these buried towns was uncovered; relief measures (Chapter 2) were directed towards resettlement elsewhere, and not, as it turned out, to excavation or reconstruction. Yet in the very first days after the eruption, before the shell had completely hardened everywhere, some attempts had been made to rescue objects from the stricken area. Nothing of this kind was done at Herculaneum, where there could be no grounds for hope. But at Pompeii parties of survivors, with the roofs of the buried buildings to guide them, dug down and recovered a certain amount of jewellery, furniture, money and documents; and many statues and marble facings in the Forum were also unearthed and removed.

The rescue parties have left graffiti; or perhaps these are the work of robbers looking for loot. 'Broken into,' records one such inscription (written in the Latin language, but with Greek letters) – though at this particular point a valuable statue was left behind. Elsewhere appears a sinister verse; 'There were fifty of them, still lying where they had been.' And sometimes a moral note is struck. 'The cup from which the whore poured her libation is now covered by stones and ashes.' 'Sodom and Gomorrah' is what another man has written: perhaps he was a Jew or a Christian.[1] So-called Sibylline Oracles circulating in the east, under Jewish inspiration, declared that the holocaust was a divine punishment on the emperor Titus, who had sacked Jerusalem.[2] And the writer of a papyrus recently discovered in Egypt, *The Apocalypse of Adam*, has this catastrophe in mind (and perhaps Pliny's account of it) when he prophesies a terrible rain of fire, pumice and asphalt.[3] The Roman poets of the day expressed their horror at what had happened. Jupiter, says Statius – himself a Neapolitan – had torn out the entrails of Vesuvius, lifted them up to the stars, and cast them down again upon the victims. But to Martial it seemed that even the gods would not have dared to do anything as dreadful as this.[4]

A millennium and a half later, in 1594, Count Muzio Tuttavilla had the idea of diverting the river Sarno to his villa near the sea at Torre Annunziata. As workmen dug the underground channel they encountered ancient walls covered with paintings and inscriptions; and to these discoveries they drew the attention of the architect in charge, Domenico Fontana. One of the inscriptions referred to a town councillor at Pompeii *(decurio Pompeiis)*, but the significant fact that it gave the name of the hitherto unidentified ancient site was missed. In 1709 began the disastrous tunnellings of D'Elboeuf at Herculaneum (Chapter 3). Then, in 1738, more regular excavations started at the site, enabling Horace Walpole to detect 'perhaps one of the noblest curiosities that has ever been discovered. There is nothing of the kind known in the world.' In 1775 the Herculaneum Academy was founded, and two years later, with a subsidy from King Charles of Sicily and Naples (later Charles III of Spain), the Academicians began to produce their publications, including the discoveries in the Villa of the Papyri.

Meanwhile, excavations had also begun in Pompeii when, in 1748, a Spanish engineer officer, Roque de Alcubierre, inspecting Fontana's channel, deduced that these were traces of a vast site. And so, enrolling twenty-four diggers – including twelve convicts – he made the first spade cuts above the Temple of Fortuna Augusta. On 20 August 1763 an inscription referring to 'the commonwealth of the Pompeians' *(respublica Pompeianorum)* enabled the site to be identified.

The impact of all these discoveries on the artists of western Europe was not as substantial as might have been expected.[5] The best known painter to follow

A statue of a woman, more than life-size, from the Street of the Tombs, Pompeii. Now in the Pompeii Museum

the ancient paintings at all closely was the second-rate A.R. Mengs, who deceived the archaeologist Johann Winckelmann, prophet and visionary of Neo-Classicism, into the belief that the mawkish *Jupiter and Ganymede* (1758–9), painted by himself, was an ancient original. J.-M. Vien's adaptation of *The Cupid Seller* from Stabiae (1763) supplements the first-century painting (Chapter 4) by adding simpering sentiment and an obscene gesture.[6] But, in contrast to these frivolities by painters, the impact of Pompeii and Herculaneum upon the archaeological world was enormous. The efforts of the Herculaneum Academy were augmented by the influential letters of Winckelmann. These epistles, starting in 1762, annoyed the Bourbons, who reigned at Naples, by their critical attitude; but they alerted the outside world.

'It is work which should employ three thousand men,' declared the twenty-year-old Emperor Joseph of Austria seven years later. 'There is nothing like it in Europe or Asia or Africa or America!' Among those who showed him round the site was the enlightened Sir William Hamilton, British envoy at Naples, noted as an intrepid climber of Vesuvius in eruption (Chapter 2). Hamilton bought numerous objects from Pompeii and Herculaneum for his own collection, but later had to sell a good many of them 'because he had spent so much on Emma', subsequently his wife and Nelson's mistress. Goethe never forgot the time when he had visited the region at the age of thirty-eight, and wrote about his experiences with deep feeling many years later. To him Pompeii came to symbolize the greatest of all his loves, the common denominator of his whole personality – the classical world.[7]

When the first discoveries had been made, the objects were lodged at Portici between Naples and Herculaneum, in the royal palace which was gradually constructed from 1739 onwards. In 1790, however, in

View of an eruption from the sea

order to find room for the ever-increasing treasures, the first steps were taken to remodel the building in Naples itself that is now the National Archaeological Museum.[8] Meanwhile excavations at Pompeii and Herculaneum continued during the Napoleonic 'Parthenopean Republic' (1799), gaining strength under Murat (1806–15) and during the first decade or two of the Bourbon restoration which followed. Giacomo Leopardi deplored the concealment of so much of Herculaneum beneath the modern town of Resina. Madame de Staël's romance-travelogue *Corinne ou l'Italie* (1807), which has been summed up as the worst great novel ever written, deals extensively with Pompeii; and the 'House of Glaucus', described by Bulwer Lytton in *The Last Days of Pompeii* (1834), is closely modelled upon the House of the Tragic Poet. This famous romance, which was inspired by a visit to the site and by a picture he had seen in Milan, was perhaps also owed, in part, to a suggestion from Marguerite (Lady) Blessington, a famous beauty (painted by Lawrence) who knew the region well and later wrote *The Idler in Italy;* and Lytton obtained much of his information from the popular *Pompeiana* of the distinguished traveller Sir William Gell, to whom the book is dedicated. In the same year as Lytton's novel, Joseph Méry of Marseilles wrote a poem about the downfall of Herculaneum, which he later converted into the libretto of an opera with music by Félicien David.

Ludwig of Bavaria, who constantly visited Pompeii, built an imitation of the House of the Dioscuri at Aschaffenburg. Another visitor was Sir Walter Scott (1833), who repeated the words *City of the Dead* over and over again: and then Queen Victoria came in 1838. 'The place is charming with its ruins,' said Maximilian, the future emperor of Mexico (1851), 'but also terrible. Like painted corpses the little rooms still glitter in their garish colours.'[9]

The desolate scene in the Atrio di Cavallo, between the two peaks of Vesuvius, after the eruption of 1897

In the year of revolutions (1848), Guiseppe Fiorelli had trained his twenty archaeological diggers as artillerymen; and for a time he was placed under arrest. But from 1864 onwards,[10] after the unification of the Neapolitan Kingdom with Italy, he was curator, and his excavations achieved a new high standard of systematic discipline – in addition to winning great fame or notoriety because of the technique he had invented for reconstructing dead bodies by plaster casts (Chapter 2). An effort by Charles Waldstein (Sir Charles Walston) to promote an international scheme for the excavation of Herculaneum came to nothing (1904). Subsequently, however, nearly forty years of work by the distinguished Italian archaeologist Amedeo Maiuri, from 1924 at Pompeii and from 1927 at Herculaneum, registered immense progress and marked improvements of method, including the use of electric boring machines and mechanical shovels. Maiuri displayed a determination to retain as many of his discoveries as possible on the spot, instead of removing them to museums, since he wanted to give an accurate picture of what the ancient houses and buildings had actually looked like at various periods of their development.[11] About three-fifths of Pompeii have now been uncovered, but a smaller proportion of Herculaneum, where work is encumbered with greater difficulties.

In 1940 Mussolini entertained the German Minister of Education, Bernhard Rust, in the dining-room of the House of Menander; and Felix Hartlaub, in his *Tagebuch aus dem Kriege*, found himself reminded of Pompeii on an occasion when he was moving into the hastily evacuated government offices of an overrun enemy: they looked as if time had come to a stop. At Pompeii, however, at this period, this suspension of time was no longer complete, for in August and September 1943 pilots of the Allied air forces dropped 162 bombs on the place. Their bombing badly damaged the Houses of the Faun and the Moralist and wrecked the museum, but disclosed beneath it the Villa of the Marine Gate; and as a result of the same operations the suburban Temple of Dionysus also came to light (Chapters 4, 5).[12] When the Allied offensive at Monte Cassino started early in the following year, sixty cases full of ancient gold, silver and glass objects – mainly products of the various excavations on the Vesuvian sites, which had been stored at the monastery since the previous June – were only just removed in time. Meanwhile, a fortnight previously, Vesuvius itself had threatened to compete by starting its most recent eruption (Chapter 2).

And now what there is left to do, in the words of Maiuri, is 'a complex, laborious, arduous, slow and costly work of preservation, protection and restoration'. But there also remains, without a doubt, the certainty of immense and remarkable future discoveries – especially at Herculaneum. Beneath the volcanic mud there must still be ancient objects which could eclipse in splendour, beauty and interest almost any relic of antiquity that has been found anywhere in the world. Other ancient periods, other places, may nowadays seem more urgently in need of attention, because interest has shifted to prehistoric societies. But the civilization of Rome, too, is still capable of yielding many rewarding secrets, which may well throw much-needed light not only on the remaining enigmas of the ancient world but on the origins of our own society which owes that world so much. And Pompeii and Herculaneum, as in the past, are the places from which this new illumination can come.

Meanwhile the archaeologists, at these two places, are continuing their work. This book has tried to show the marvels their predecessors have given the world. There are surely further marvels to come.

The Via degli Augustali, Pompeii

Maps and Plans

Notes

1: THE HISTORY OF POMPEII AND HERCULANEUM

1. The northern boundary of Campania was Sinuessa, according to the early imperial geographers; earlier it had been at the Aurunci Mountains. Under Diocletian the territory was extended to include the whole of Latium, part of which has consequently received the name of the 'Roman Campagna'. To the south, beyond the Surrentine spur, the Ager Picentinus (Bay of Salerno) was excluded from Campania by Pliny, but often it was included. The main rivers of Campania were the Liris (Garigliano) (174 km), and in the main plain the Vulturnus (166 km).

2. If, as is uncertain, a lemon should be identified in a painting at the House of the Orchard, Pompeii, it was an exotic rarity.

3. Pliny, *Natural History*, III, 40; Florus 1, 11, 3

4. Strabo, v, 4, 8.

5. Cf. burials at Striano, Torio, S. Marzano, S. Valentino. There was also a necropolis close to the coast near Castellamare di Stabia, and another at Gragnano.

6. It did not come from *campus* as was believed in antiquity. The word appears with Oscan terminations on coins of the fifth or fourth century BC. At first the phrase *Campanus ager* was used; 'Campania' became common only in the first century AD.

7. Apparently from *pompe* meaning 'five' – perhaps a personal name. The order of the Oscan alphabet (twenty-one letters) is shown by fragments of alphabets at Pompeii. The Campanians under Samnite rule were known as 'Osci'. In the first century BC Roman antiquarians used the word 'Sabelli' to cover Samnites and other speakers of Oscan-type dialects.

8. The official was the *meddis tovtiks* or *meddix tuticus*, and the word used for the Assembly is *kombennio-* or *komparakio-*.

9. For Pompeii see Appian, *Civil Wars*, 1, 39.

10. *Corpus Inscriptionum Latinarum*, IV, 5385.

11. In the managers of farm estates the names of pre-Sullan Pompeians continue to predominate.

12. Cicero, *For Sulla*, 21, 61. The disputes concerned public walks and voting.

13. Appian, *Civil Wars*, 1, 89.

14. The view that Nero then founded a new colony is based on an inconclusive inscription (*Corpus Inscriptionum Latinarum*, IV, 3525).

2: VESUVIUS

1. Strabo, v, 4 and 247. But it has been suggested that strata overlaying graves of the eighth century BC indicate that eruptions had taken place since then. Vesuvius is the intermediate type of volcano, not permanently active but liable to erupt explosively at times.

2. Virgil, *Georgics*, II, 224.

3. In the House of Bacchus at Pompeii, and at Herculaneum. There is no need to suppose that their depiction of a single cone is merely conventional.

4. For the date of Tacitus, *Annals*, XV, 22, 5, against Seneca, *Natural Questions*, VI, 2 (AD 63) (which may be an interpolation). Tacitus' date is indirectly confirmed by Seneca, *op. cit.*, VI, 1, 13.

5. Seneca, *op. cit.*, VI, 27, 1 f.

6. Evidence from crops etc. denies the alternative dating to 23 November given in later codices of the younger Pliny and in the first printed edition.

7. The younger Pliny, *Letters*, VI, 16, 4–20 (trans. B. Radice).

8. Valerius Flaccus, *Argonautica*, III, 208 ff., Dio Cassius, *Epitome*, LXVI, 22, 4. Dio's further statement, however, that the people were assembled in the amphitheatre when the disaster struck – a dramatic godsend to Bulwer Lytton and other novelists and film-writers – is extremely improbable; and no traces of bodies have been found there.

9. The younger Pliny, *Letters*, VI, 20, 6, 8–9, 16 (trans. B. Radice). Pliny does not seem, after all, to have made for the house of Rectina (wife of Cn. Pedius Cascus, consul 71), which must have become inaccessible before he could get there.

10. Suetonius, *Titus*, 8, 3 f.

11. Dio Cassius, *Epitome*, LXXVII, 2, 1.

3: THE TOWNS AND THEIR MEETING PLACES

1. Cicero, *On the Agrarian Law*, II, 35, 95 f. The houses at Pompeii have their short sides facing the street, in contrast to Greek cities such as Olynthus at Macedonia, where the long sides are in this position.

2. But some stones had to be removed in 1815 to let the coach of the Queen of Naples pass.

3. The building of tombs outside the Nola Gate was also proceeding in 79.

4. Petronius, *Satyricon*, 71 (trans. J. Sullivan).

5. The land here has sunk in relation to the sea, the ancient surface being nearly two metres below the present sea-level.

6. Vitruvius, V, 1, 1, 7.

7. There is also a fine four-fronted arch on the main street (Decumanus Maximus) at Herculaneum.

8. Gaius Pumidius Diphilus scratched his name on the wall on 3 October 78 BC.

9. Basilicas vary in this respect, having their entrances at the short end at Rome, Corinth and Lepcis Magna, and on the long sides (according to the Vitruvian canon) at Fanum, Cosa and Sabrata.

10. Tacitus, *Annals*, XIV, 17 (trans. M. Grant).

11. Nicolaus of Damascus, *fragment* 78 (F. Jacoby, *Fragmente der griechischen Historiker*, II A,378). Cf. M. Grant, *Gladiators*, pp. 79, 96.

12. *Corpus Inscriptionum Latinarum*, IV, 4418.

13. Not Bovianum Vetus, as suggested; there was probably no such place.

14. This sort of figure was known as an Atlas, a Telamon or a Persian.

15. Some are now in Dresden and Vienna.

16. The round temple at Tibur (Tivoli) might have had a concrete dome at an earlier date, though its existence has been doubted. The Pompeian dome is externally square, and internally circular except for a curved niche. The main lines of the imperial installations in Rome were worked out during the first century AD, the Baths of Nero fulfilling a prominent role.

17. Cf. R.E.M. Wheeler, *Roman Art and Architecture*, London, 1964, pp. 146 f.; in the painting at the Villa of the Mysteries (*ibid.*, fig. 128) there is a broken architrave.

18. The elder Pliny, *Natural History*, IX, 68.

19. *Ibid.*, XXVIII, 191; made of beech ashes and goat's tallow (or hornbeam if *carpineo* is a better reading than *caprineo*).

20. Juvenal, *Satires*, VII, 129 f. (trans. P. Green).

21. Seneca, *Moral Letters*, LVI, 1 ff.

To complete this chapter, it must be added that private persons, such as Julia Felix and Crassus Frugi, also let out or organized bathing facilities: see Chapter 7.

4: TEMPLES; GODS AND GODDESSES; AND PHILOSOPHERS

1. Though there is a shrine of the emperors in the *Collegium* of the Priests of Augustus *(Augustales)*. There are no signs yet of the Temple of the Mother of the Gods, restored by Vespasian *(Corpus Inscriptionum Latinarum*, X, 1406).

2. Three capitals of the early temple have survived, and terracotta fittings. In Roman times it was reduced to a small shrine. Possibly by then it had been rededicated to another cult.

3. Apollo was 'Actius' because he had presided over the victory at Actium. Paintings of sea-battles in Pompeii may refer to this engagement: e.g. M. Grant, *Nero*, p. 63.

4. *Corpus Inscriptionum Latinarum*, IV, 1824.

5. Lucretius, I, 1 ff. (trans. B. Bunting).

6. *Corpus Inscriptionum Latinarum*, IV, 1520, 6865, X, 928.

7. The theory of Etruscan origin is disputed. But the Pompeian temple was oriented to the points of the compass in the Etruscan fashion.

8. At Athens the cult related to the underworld, and was often symbolized by a snake.

9. Recent excavations have revealed a whole workshop of magical practices. They are also depicted in paintings (e.g. wayfarer and witch in the House of the Dioscuri), and mosaics (sorceress with women clients, Chapter 6), and there are many spells against the evil eye. The 'magic square' found at the House of Paquius Proculus and upon a column of the Large Palaestra beside the amphitheatre (1936) is not necessarily Christian, as has been supposed; nor, in all probability, is the cross-like shape on a stuccoed wall in the House of the Bicentenary at Herculaneum (1939). But if there is no firm evidence for Christians at Pompeii, there were numerous Jews, including a wine-merchant, Abinnericus, and a bar maid, Maria; advertisements refer to the Jewish diet, and graffiti to the practice of circumcision.

10. Apuleius, *Metamorphoses*, XI, 1, 3.

11. A metope of local stone (found in 1953) showing the punishment of Ixion on a wheel for attempting to violate Juno (the theme also of a painting in the House of the Vettii) seems to have formed part of another Samnite temple.

12. Stabiae: Villa of the Cupid-Seller (Chapter 5). Stucco relief: M. Grant, *Nero*, p. 188.

13. Cf. P. MacKendrick, *The Mute Stones Speak*, pp. 220 f. A leading part in the worship of Dionysus-Bacchus was played by children. The figure with the whip has been variously identified as Justice, Victory, a Fury and Shame (Aidos).

14. G. Zunz, 'On the Dionysiac Fresco in the Villa dei Misteri at Pompeii', *Proceedings of the British Academy*, XLIX, 1963, p. 174. Zunz believes that some figures have been added by local artists to the original plan.

15. Petronius, *Satyricon*, 41. In the Temple of Apollo at Pompeii there was a painting of Bacchus brandishing his staff and pouring wine.

16. Petronius, *op. cit.*, 35 (trans. J. Sullivan).

17. Graffito on wall next to the House of Gaius Julius Polybius (trans. K. and R. Gregor Smith in E. C. Corti, *The Destruction and Resurrection of Pompeii and Herculaneum*, 1951).

18. Cf. Philodemus, *Epigrams*, XXIII, (3302 ff.); Cicero, *For Sestius*, 94, *On the Consular Provinces*, 7.

19. Philodemus, *Epigrams*, VIII (3206 ff.) (trans. K. Rexroth).

20. *Ibid.*, XIII (3236 ff.) (trans. D. Fitts). Fitts (though not Philodemus) ends the poem with another line: 'Are you a lover or a Senator'?

5: PRIVATE HOUSES IN TOWN AND COUNTRY

1. F. E. Brown, *Roman Architecture*, p. 14.
2. Beneath the House of the Faun there are traces of a building of the early third century BC.
3. By a close investigation of inscriptions found on the sites, Professor M. della Corte discovered the homes of more than five hundred identifiable inhabitants of Pompeii. Of the post-classical names the least relevant is 'House of Aristides' at Herculaneum, so called because in the eighteenth century this building was crossed by the tunnels to the Villa of the Papyri, in which one statue was erroneously believed to represent Aristides.
4. Perhaps it was built for the Arriani Polliani. Later it belonged to Marcus Nigidius Vaccula.
5. But the House of the Beautiful Courtyard, for example, has no *fauces*. Virgil uses both terms in describing the entrance to the underworld.
6. The opening and basin are known as *compluvium* and *impluvium* respectively; but the terms can also be interchanged.
7. Petronius, *Satyricon*, 29; Plautus, *Aulularia*, 23 ff. Dozens of *lararia* have vanished since their discovery.
8. The forms of these tables followed Hellenistic patterns: large marble table supports of the second century BC have been found at Pergamum.
9. The owners of this house were Marcus Epidius Hymenaeus and Gaius Arrius Crescens.
10. The absence of a chimney is confirmed by the way the stove is built in the kitchen of the House of Augustus on the Palatine Hill at Rome, though a bakery at Pompeii seems to have had a pipe which served as a sort of chimney (Chapter 7). In rich houses, especially of an early date, there could be a *pistrinum* (bakehouse and mill) near the kitchen.
11. House of the Faun, House of Caecilius Jucundus, Villa of Diomede.
12. Varro, *De Re Rustica*, III, 7.
13. E.g. at Silchester (Reading Museum).
14. The younger Pliny, *Letters*, IX, 36, 1.
15. Several villas at Boscoreale show particularly remarkable sets of baths.
16. Trans. J. Lindsay, *The Writing on the Wall*, London, 1960, p. 108. The copper-smith Verus, in the Via dell'Abbondanza, sold chamber-pots as well as surveyors' instruments.
17. E.g. Pompeii, Regio I, Insula 10, No. 11. Very occasionally it is an arcade not a colonnade, e.g. in the House of Decimus Caprasius Felix (IX.7.20).
18. It was called a villa and not a house, because its first discoverers in 1755-7 did not know that it was inside the walls; and it looked like a country villa. The building was re-excavated in 1952 and 1953.
19. Philodemus, *Epigrams*, XX (3280 ff.) (trans. K. Rexroth). For 'sprouts' read 'cabbage-stalks'.
20. Cicero, *Letters to Atticus*, XIV, 9, 1.
21. The walls between the old houses were also abolished by linking passages and stairways.
22. E.g. the house within the School of Trajan.
23. Strabo, V, 4, 8. Boccaccio described the region as 'full of little cities, of gardens, of fountains and of rich men'.
24. The identification of a 'Villa of Cicero', outside the Herculaneum Gate, is purely conjectural. Villa of Agrippa Postumus: *Corpus Inscriptionum Latinarum*, IV, 6499, 6995. Caligula and Agrippina: Seneca, *On Anger*, III, 21, 5. Trimalchio: Petronius, *Satyricon*, 53.
25. Country mansions are known as *villae urbanae*, and when they are associated with large-scale agricultural workshops they are sometimes called *pseudo-urbanae*.
26. *Corpus Inscriptionum Latinarum*, IV, 9226.
27. The Villa, at the Fondo Gaspare di Martino, owes its name to a painting found there, which became famous in the eighteenth century (see Epilogue). It is also known as the Villa Ariadne, from another painting.
28. Also known as the 'Edificio Porticato' (at San Marco, Fondo Fratelli dello Ioio).
29. Among numerous other discoveries in the area, the bath of a villa of the 70s AD has now been found in the adjoining plain.
30. Such towers were perhaps survivals of earlier fortified country-houses, e.g. the mansion of the elder Scipio Africanus at Liternum in Campania.
31. *Journal of Roman Studies*, London, 1965, p. 162
32. Horace, *Odes*, III, 1, 33-7 (trans. Lord Dunsany).

6: PAINTINGS, MOSAICS AND FURNITURE

1. G. M. A. Richter, *A Handbook of Greek Art*, 6th ed., 1969, p. 285. The term 'fresco' is not altogether appropriate because of the possibilities of retouching; cf M. Brion, *Pompeii and Herculaneum*, London, 1960, p. 209.
2. Polychrome vases of the third century BC from Centuripe in Sicily are also relevant, cf. Richter, *op. cit.*, pp. 279, 363 f., 366.
3. Egypt: Suk-el-Wardian, Anfushy. Delos also shows stucco imitations of white marble blocks (late third and early second centuries BC).
4. The style began between 80 and 70 BC, and its termination is various attributed to *c*. 50 BC, 1 BC and AD 14. In the entrance of the Samnite House at Herculaneum, there are two Second Style landscape panels above First Style Paintings.
5. Vitruvius, V, 6, 8; V, 8, 1; VII, 5, 2.
6. When the elder Pliny blames the scene-painter Apaturius of Alabanda for fantastic architectural motifs at the theatre at Tralles (Aydin), it is disputed whether he is referring to this 'Second' or to the subsequent 'Third' style. Or perhaps he is blaming both.
7. Tombs at Sidi Gaber; papyrus discovered by C. Nordenfalk (1951).

8. Third-century attempts at perspective: e.g. stele of Hediste from Pagasae in Thessaly (Volo museum). 'Scientific' painting had started *c.* 400 BC: Vitruvius, *op. cit.*, VII, *preface*, 2; Hesychius, s.v. *Skia;* the elder Pliny, *Natural History*, XXXV, 60 f; Quintilian, *Institutio Oratoria*, XII, 10, 4.

9. A fourth-century AD manuscript of the *Eclogues* (Vatican no. 3225) is illustrated by just this sort of landscape.

10. *Natural History*, XXXV, 116f.

11. If Vitruvius, V, 6, 9, refers to 'topiary art', *opus topiarium*, garden landscape was already used in stage scenery as early as 30 BC.

12. Petronius, *Satyricon*, 46.

13. Vitruvius, VI, 7, 4.

14. The elder Pliny, *Natural History*, XXXV, 112.

15. Variously dated from *c.* 20 BC or 1, or AD 14 to *c.* AD 20 or 50 or 63. Regarded by some as a subdivision of the Second Style.

16. Painted in encaustic, i.e. with the application of heated beeswax. On the obscurities of this technique see A.F. Shore, *Portrait Painting from Roman Egypt*, pp. 22 ff.

17. A simpler version without the architecture (end of Third Style) comes from the House of Lucius Caecilius Jucundus. The original was probably of *c.* 330–320 BC. For the design at Herculaneum resembling a stage set see M. Grant, *The World of Rome*, plate 45 (c).

18. Cf. last note, and the fine *Theseus and the Athenian Captives* (from the Basilica at Herculaneum), of which an inferior version was found at the House of Gavius Rufus at Pompeii. The original of both was perhaps a painting by Euphranor (fourth century BC). Paintings illustrating the story of Theseus have also now been found at the House of the Cupid Seller, Stabiae. It is very rare to find paintings like the *Three Graces* (from Pompeii) which is a fairly exact copy of a well-known model.

19. M. Grant, *Myths of the Greeks and Romans*, pl. 76.

20. *The Fall of Icarus* from the House of Amandus at Pompeii (ibid. pl. 89), showing two successive stages of the action, was another theme Nero was interested in (its enactment before him in a dramatic performance ended in disaster, M. Grant, *Nero*, p. 84).

21. *Iphigenia* (*Nero*, p. 93) is after Timanthes or Pheimantes, *c.* 400 BC; and *Achilles and Briseis* from Apelles, *c.* 330–25.

22. Petronius, *Satyricon*, 89 (trans. W. Arrowsmith). For the painting see also *Nero*, pp. 190–1.

23. In the House of Apollo there is a painting of an Egyptian landscape with non-Egyptian figures.

24. A.J.P. Wace, 'Il tappeto nell'antichità', *Archeologica Classica*, 1969, pp. 72–7.

25. So-called because first supposed to have been used at Signia (Segni) in Latium.

26. Or perhaps Aristides of Thebes. The two painters had the same master, Nicomachus.

27. Sosus: Pliny, *Natural History*, XXXVII, 184. The 'unswept floor', illustrated in *Nero*, p. 193, is found not only in Italy but at Aquileia and in North Africa. The Vatican example was formerly in the Museo Profano Lateranense.

28. A.F. Shore, *Portrait Painting from Roman Egypt*, pl. 2.

29. Pollux, X, 42, cf. Richter, *A Handbook of Greek Art*, 6th ed., p. 280.

30. The most recently found examples are from the House of Marcus Fabius Rufus at the north-western end of Pompeii (1961–2).

31. Cf. also tripods in J.L. David's portrait of Madame Récamier. He had arranged for actual tripods to be made, both for use and for studio props after *c.* 1785. But they were regarded as extraordinary at the time; direct imitation remained rare during the eighteenth century and was restricted to surface detail, H. Honour, *Neo-Classicism*, pp. 47 ff.

32. The owners of the house seem to have included Lucius Caecilius Aphrodisius, Tiberius Claudius Amphio (does his Claudian name mean that he was an imperial freedman and that this was an imperial property?) and Lucius Brittius Eros.

7: FARMS AND TRADES

1. Fondo Vincenzo di Prisco (discovered 1893–4). Cf. D.S. Robertson, *Greek and Roman Architecture*, 1969 ed., p. 311.

2. The Epidian family had a whole separate cemetery for their slaves.

3. Other villas at Positano (which meant the estate of the Posidii), across the Monti Lattari (Lactarii) due south of Stabiae, still remain to be excavated. On the peninsula of Surrentum alone, eighteen villas of various kinds had already been located in 1946.

4. Pagus Saliniensis, Campaniensis, Urbulanensis.

5. Since 1957 there have been excavations at nearby S. Maria delle Grazie and at Retraro, where a villa has yielded forty-two stucco fragments.

6. A certain Marcus Crassus Frugi also advertised his privately owned baths, with 'sea-water and bathing in soft water'.

7. A Vettius is known by an inscription to have been a priest of the imperial cult, i.e. an *Augustalis* (see Chapter 4), which suggests that he was a freedman.

8. Vesuvian wine was praised by Florus, 1, 16.

9. Columella, III, 2, 27. It was also called Murgentina. The same sort of wine was made in larger quantities at Clusium (Chiusi).

10. The elder Pliny, *Natural History*, XIV, 70.

11. *Corpus Inscriptionum Latinarum*, IV, 6867–9.

12. E.g. Inn of Hedone: 4 *asses* (1 *sestertius*); other brands 1 and 2 *asses*.

13. Cf. also types of stone found at Nola and Suessa Aurunca.

14. A few of these had a pipe resembling a chimney (usually absent in houses, Chapter 5): one pipe seems to go up to a drying cupboard on the first floor.

15. Wool was dyed in the fleece; silk, cotton and linen in the thread.

16. E.g. in the corner-wall of the Via dell'Abbondanza near the House of Julius Polybius.

17. Now at the Museum of Fine Art, Boston, and in the Castello at Nocera Inferiore.

18. *Geoponica*, xx, 46, 1; cf. M. Ponsich and M. Tarradell, *Garum et Industries Antiques de salaison dans la Méditerranée Occidentale*, Paris, 1965.

19. Martial, *Epigrams*, VII, 94.

20. The roses of the Phlegraean Fields, north of Neapolis, supplied the perfumeries of Capua.

21. E.g. two boxes of the best products of La Graufesenque ware.

22. Cf. Tcherma, *Mémoires de l'Ecole Française à Rome*, LXXVI, Paris, 1964, pp. 419 ff.

23. The coins of Ebusus are also found elsewhere in Campania.

24. Another important find consisted of eighteen wax tablets, in triplicate, in the House of the Bicentenary (Herculaneum); they are legal documents relating to one of the tenants, Gaius Petronius Stephanus.

8: PUBLIC LIFE AND SEXUAL LIFE

1. Petronius, *Satyricon*, 44 (trans. J. Sullivan).

2. Trans. J. Lindsay, *The Writing on the Wall*, London, 1960, p. 36.

3. They were two men called Pompeius and Grosphus, replaced not only by two *duoviri* but by a special *praefectus iure dicundo*, Sextus Pompeius Proculus.

4. And can a supporter of Gaius Cuspius Pansa really be called Fabius Multitremulus, as an inscription records?

5. Philodemus, *On Vices* (including character-sketches by Ariston of Ceos).

6. Another such head, belonging to an equestrian statue of Marcus Nonius Balbus, was blown off by a cannon-ball which hit the royal palace at Portici (see Epilogue) during civil strife in 1799. It was reconstructed and is now, like the other heads, in the Archaeological Museum at Naples.

7. 'Sabina' (*Corpus Inscriptionum Latinarum*, IV, 9171, etc.) may also be the empress, whose full name was Poppaea Sabina.

8. C. Vermeule, *Antike Kunst*, I, 6, 1963, p. 39. Inscription at Villa of Agrippa Postumus: *Corpus Inscriptionum Latinarum*, IV, 6893.

9. Trans. P. MacKendrick, *The Mute Stones Speak*, p. 212.

10. Trans. J. Lindsay, *op. cit.*, p. 162.

11. Julius Speratus can only record that he finds nothing so beautiful as his home-town Puteoli.

12. 16 *asses* (Attike), or 12; or even 1.

13. Trans. J. Lindsay, *op. cit.*, p. 161.

14. *Epigrams*, XII, 61.

EPILOGUE

1. 'There were fifty': House of the Golden Cupids. 'Sodom': found by A. Mau in 1885 and now lost.

2. *Oracula Sibyllina*, IV.

3. H. Goedicke, *American Journal of Philology*, 1969, p. 341. Found at Nag Hammadi.

4. Statius, *Silvae*, V, 3, 207 f.; Martial, *Epigrams*, IV, 44.

5. The styles of interior decoration of Adam, Cameron, etc., went back rather to Raphael's *Loggia* (Giovanni da Udine etc.), i.e. eventually to Nero's Golden House. Mr Hugh Honour has suggested to me that the debts of Boucher and Fragonard to Pompeian paintings might be a fruitful study, and that reliefs of *putti* (Cupids) in the Palazzo Altieri at Rome are based on paintings in the House of the Vettii.

6. J. L. David made a drawing from a print of the same painting in the late 1770s.

7. In 1830 Goethe's son was present at the excavation of the House of the Faun, known also as the House of Goethe.

8. The finds were finally lodged there by 1822. The museum became state property in 1860. Its name has now been changed from the National Museum to the National Archaeological Museum, since there are other National Museums in Naples.

9. Later, the Empress Elizabeth often came to Naples and Pompeii, and had casts made of two bronze athletes from the Villa of the Papyri, Herculaneum, for her palace the Achilleion at Corfu.

10. Alexander Dumas, senior, was the more or less honorary director of the Naples Museum and Pompeii from 1860–4, attended by 'a very charming midshipwoman who does duty in the yacht in a dapper jacket and trousers'.

11. Until the 1920s the aim had simply been to preserve the town as it had been in AD 79.

12. The somewhat complex circumstances of the raids are described by A. Maiuri, *Pompei ed Ercolano: tra case e abitanti*.

Bibliography

A Brief Bibliography

J.H. d'Arms, *Romans on the Bay of Naples*, Harvard, 1970

M.D'Avino, *The Women of Pompeii*, Naples, 1967

J.P.V.D. Balsdon, *Life and Leisure in Ancient Rome*, London, 1969

G. Becatti, *L'arte romana*, Milan, 1962

G. Becatti, *Pitture murali campane*, Florence, 1955

H.G. Beyen, *Die Pompejanische Wanddekoration vom zweiten bis zum vierten Stil*, The Hague, I, 1938; II, 1960

A. Boethius and J. B. Ward-Perkins, *Etruscan and Roman Architecture*, Harmondsworth, 1970

M. Brion, *Pompeii and Herculaneum: The Glory and the Grief*, London, 1960

A.W. van Buren, *A Companion to the Study of Pompeii and Herculaneum*, 2nd ed., Rome, 1938

A.W. van Buren, in Pauly-Wissowa-Kroll, *Real-encyclopädie der classischen Altertumswissenschaften*, vol XXI, 2 (1952), columns 1999–2038, s.v. Pompeii

J. Carcopino, *La vie quotidienne à Rome à l'apogée de l'empire*, Paris, 1938 (English ed.: *Daily Life in Ancient Rome*, Harmondsworth, 1962)

R.C. Carrington, *Pompeii*, Clarendon Press, Oxford, 1936

P. Ciprotti, *Conoscere Pompei*, Rome, 1959

M. della Corte, *Case ed abitanti di Pompei*, 2nd ed., Rome, 1965

E.C. Corti, *Untergang und Auferstehung von Pompeji und Herculaneum*, 6th ed., Munich, 1944 (English ed.: *The Death and Resurrection of Herculaneum and Pompeii*, London, 1951)

J.M. Croisille, *Les natures mortes Campaniennes* (Coll. Latomus LXXVI), Brussels, 1965

C.M. Dawson, *Roman-Campanian Mythological Landscape Painting* (Yale Classical Studies IX), Newhaven, 1944; reprint, 1965

J.J. Deiss, *Herculaneum*, New York, London, 1966

E. Diehl, *Pompejanische Wandinschriften*, 2nd ed., Berlin, 1930

H. Drerup, *Die römische villa*, Marburger Winckelmann-Programm, 1959

O. Elia, *Pitture di Stabia*, Naples, 1957

R. Etienne, *La vie quotidienne à Pompéi*, Paris, 1966

A. de Franciscis, *Pompeii-Herculaneum: Guide with Reconstructions*, Rome, 1964

M.M. Gabriel, *Masters of Campanian Painting*, New York, 1952

A. van Gerkan, *Stadtplan von Pompeji*, Berlin, 1940

M. Gigante, *Ricerche Filodemee*, Naples, 1969

P. Grimal, *Les jardins romains de la fin de la République aux deux premièrers siècles de l'Empire*, Paris, 1943

C.M. Havelock, *Hellenistic Art*, New York, 1969

S.A. and W.F. Jashemski, *Pompeii*, New York, 1965

E. Kusch, *Herculaneum*, Nuremberg, 1970

W. Leppmann, *Pompeji: Eine Stadt in Literatur und Leben* (English ed.: *Pompeii in Fact and Fiction*, London, 1968)

J. Lindsay, *The Writing on the Wall*, London, 1960

A.G. McKay, *Greek and Roman Domestic Architecture*, London, 1972

A. Maiuri, *Herculaneum and the Villa of the Papyri*, Novara, 1963

A. Maiuri, *Pompei ed Ercolano: tra case e abitanti*, Padua, 1951; Milan, 1958

A. Maiuri, *Pompei, Ercolano e Stabia*, Novara, 1961

B. Maiuri, *Il Museo Nazionale di Napoli*, Naples, 1954

A. Mau and A. Ippel, *Führer durch Pompeji*, 6th ed., Leipzig, 1928

G.G. Oncrato, *Iscrizioni pompeiane*, 2 vols, Florence, 1957–8

L. d'Orsi, *Gli scavi di Stabia*, Naples, 1954

U.E. Paoli, *Vita Romana*, 8th ed., Florence, 1958 (English ed.: *Rome: Its People and Customs*, London, 1963)

G. Picard, *Roman Painting*, London, 1970

G.L. Ragghianti, *Pittori di Pompei*, Milan, 1963

K. Schefold, *Die Wände Pompejis*, Berlin, 1957

K. Schefold, *Vergessenes Pompeji*, Berne, 1962

M. J. Sergejenko, *Pompeji*, 3rd ed., Leipzig, 1955

H. H. Tanzer, *The Common People of Pompeii* (Johns Hopkins University Studies in Archaeology, No. 29), Baltimore, 1939

J. M. C. Toynbee, *The Art of the Romans*, London, 1965

R. E. M. Wheeler, *Roman Art and Architecture*, London, 1964

G. Zunz, *On the Dionysiac Fresco in the Villa dei Misteri* (Proceedings of the British Academy, No. 49), Oxford, 1963

Acknowledgements

Sources of Illustrations

In addition to the photographs by Werner Forman we have made use of the following sources of illustrations, whose help and permission we gratefully acknowledge: Alinari 27, 40–1, 42–3, 78 (upper picture), 86, 93, 97, 99, 109, 114, 116, 136, 140, 150, 154, 155, 157, 158, 160, 165, 167, 168–9, 174, 175 (upper and lower pictures), 176, 187 (upper and lower pictures), 188, 200, 207, 208, 209, 212, 216, 217; Anderson 144, 198; Brogi 79, 96; Mr André Held 95, 100; Elek Books 38; Spring Books 84; Dr Libero d'Orsi 103, 166 (left and right).

Literary Sources

The author and publishers wish to thank the following for their permission to quote from the publications listed below:
The Cleaners' Press, Texas: *Poems*, Basil Bunting, 1950; Faber and Faber Ltd, *Greek Anthology*, transl. D. Fitts, 1957; Heinemann, and Curtis Brown Ltd: *The Odes of Horace*, transl. Lord Dunsany, 1947; Methuen and Co Ltd and St Martin's Press Inc: *The Mute Stones Speak*, Paul Mackendrick, 1960; Frederick Muller Ltd: *The Writing on the Wall*, Jack Lindsay, 1960; New American Library(Mentor): *Petronius: The Satyricon*, transl. W. Arrowsmith, 1959; Penguin Books Ltd: *Juvenal: The Sixteen Satires*, transl. P. Green, 1967, *The Letters of the Younger Pliny*, transl. B. Radice, 1969, *Petronius: The Satyricon*, transl. J. Sullivan, 1969, *Tacitus: Annals of Imperial Rome*, transl. M. Grant, revised edition 1971; Prentice-Hall International: *Roman Architecture*, F. E. Brown, 1961; Routledge and Kegan Paul: *The Destruction and Resurrection of Pompeii and Herculaneum*, E. C. Corti, 1951; University of Michigan Press: *Poems from the Greek Anthology*, transl. K. Rexroth, 1962.

Index